# THE LAST BALMAIN TIGERS

# THE LAST
# BALMAIN TIGERS

NICHOLAS R.W. HENNING

# TABLE OF CONTENTS

# BALMAIN TIGERS BACKGROUND

During the 1980s, the New South Wales Rugby Football League (NSWRFL) foundation club Balmain Tigers roared, appearing in the finals in 1983 and again, consecutively, from 1985 to 1989. Since their inaugural season in 1908, they had won eleven premierships, with their most recent grand final win occurring in 1969. During the 1970s, however, they were not their customary selves. They made only two finals appearances during that decade, and each culminated in a quick exit, with no grand final appearance. As the 1980s got under way and progressed, the team became a menacing force once again, which was highlighted by their two grand final appearances. They weren't quite the rulers of the jungle during the 1980s, but they were highly competitive for much of the decade.

By 1990, they started to show signs of aging, with Balmain-born inspirational captain and lock forward Wayne Pearce retiring from the game. The team appeared in the finals that year but bowed out in their qualifying/elimination game on September 1, with Manly Warringah Sea Eagles winning the game 16–0 at the Sydney Football Stadium. No Balmain player that appeared in the club's 1988 or 1989 grand final teams would still be playing for the club in 1999.

Some might say that from 1991 onward, although the club tried hard to be a league power, times had changed, and club stalwarts had noticed it. "Balmain is no longer a rugby league area. Time has caught up with the Balmain Tigers…shifting populations, changing demographics, and an influx of people into the area who come from non-[rugby] league backgrounds," said Steve Roach (with Ray Chesterton 1992, p. 158). He was a former player who had played his entire career, from 1982 to 1992, with Balmain, and as a retired player and married man with a family, he lived in the local area and had seen the club change.

From 1991 to 1993, Balmain showed some flashes of promise, but they were inconsistent winners, as they finished the regular season at twelfth of sixteen teams in 1991, tenth in 1992, and fifteenth in 1993. The top six teams qualified for the finals in 1991 and the top five in 1992 and 1993, so three consecutive years out of the finals was disappointing for Balmain and its fans, as they had in the late 1980s been familiar with the club making regular finals appearances. To make matters worse, Balmain finished the 1994 season in last place, which earned them the season's booby prize—the dreaded wooden spoon.

With the team struggling rumblings of possibly moving the club predated 1994, with Balmain hooker Ben Elias saying, "I believe the Balmain Tigers have two choices for the future: re-locate or die. My preferred option is for the Tigers to fully investigate the most radical of all the various possibilities—a move to Melbourne" (Elias with Heads 1993, p. 204). Like Roach, Elias played his entire career, which spanned from 1982 to 1994, for Balmain. Interestingly, he formally made the suggestion to take the club to Melbourne, in writing, as an active player in his 1993 autobiography, *Balmain Benny: The Stormy League Career of Ben Elias.*

Some might say Elias has a tendency for his opinion to evolve and even considerably change—and there are completely reasonable factors and circumstances that can cause this. In his autobiography, he had a very strong view regarding merging Balmain with any other club: "Amalgamation is not the answer. There is no way you're ever going to get two clubs to agree to that. Take Easts and Souths; people talk about them blending into one club at some time in the future. You can get set with me. Easts and Souths have been at each other's throats for over 85 years. They are oil and water—there's no way you'd successfully get them to mix" (Elias with Heads 1993, p. 207). Six years later, however, and also into the new century, his view regarding club mergers would be considerably different. One idea he was in favour of, even during the late 1980s, was changing Balmain's home ground from Leichhardt Oval to the more modern Parramatta Stadium, and this type of thought would result in Balmain's most radical effort to reinvent itself as Sydney Tigers for 1995, playing all their home games at Parramatta Stadium and, thus, sharing the facility with the Parramatta Eels.

Danny Munk was the chief executive officer for Balmain/Sydney Tigers, and he was also its league's club facility CEO from 1995 to 2006. Munk recalls, "The board in '94 and I think it may have started as far back as '93 were starting to feel inner-city clubs like the Tigers and Souths [Rabbitohs] were really struggling commercially...the game was changing pretty fast...the older clubs like Wests, Souths and Balmain were struggling to keep pace with clubs like the Panthers, Parramatta, and Canterbury...I think the board at that stage felt they needed to have a broader base...they were looking for a national brand and so Balmain itself was very specific while Sydney was looking at a national brand...to market the product differently" (Munk, personal interview, 2018). As a foundation club from 1908, they had always been Balmain Tigers, and such a move away from tradition was certainly immense.

Beginning in 1995, the club set about on a new journey, with aims to improve its competitiveness on the field and build a long-term future. Rugby league in Australia, though, would go through perhaps its most tempestuous period from 1995 to 1999.

CHAPTER 1

# THE TIGERS FROM 1995 TO 1998

Name changes were popular during the 1995 season, and the New South Wales Rugby League (NSWRL) (which had been the competition's name since 1984) became the Australian Rugby League (ARL) that year. It was a lot more than a name change, though, as the administration of the premiership (competition) shifted from the NSWRL to the ARL. Four new teams joined the premiership: Auckland Warriors, North Queensland Cowboys, South Queensland Crushers, and Western Reds. It was ambitious to expand the premiership to twenty teams and to have a club for the first time in New Zealand and in Western Australia (Western Reds were based in the state capital city of Perth). Canterbury-Bankstown Bulldogs became Sydney Bulldogs; Eastern Suburbs were now Sydney City Roosters; and Balmain became Sydney Tigers.

Despite their slight name changes to bring broader representation of a city rather than its suburbs, the Tigers and Roosters were both foundation clubs, and they would face off against each other in Round 1 on March 12, 1995, at Parramatta Stadium. The Roosters led 12–2 at halftime, but Sydney Tigers scored 22 points during the second half and won the game 24–18. Winning their first game was very positive, and by Round 13 the Tigers had won six of their thirteen games. From Round 14 on, however, they would lose seven consecutive games and have one more win before losing their final game of the season in Round 22, and they finished the year fifteenth of twenty teams.

Perhaps the most alarming detail about 1995 was that the average home game attendance at Parramatta Stadium was 6,530, and their biggest of the year was 9,987. Despite the Balmain Tigers finishing in last place in 1994, with just four wins for the season, their average home crowd at Leichhardt Oval that year was 7,348, and the biggest was 12,668. One season was a small sample for the Sydney Tigers to be measured on, but understanding why they were drawing less than the 1994 season warranted careful consideration.

While Sydney Tigers looked for ways to improve, the game around them was becoming volatile. A breakaway Super League (SL) competition was more than a talking point by 1995, and what became known as the Super League and Australian Rugby League war was quickly visible to all that played and followed the game, given the ineligibility of SL-aligned players to represent the New South Wales Blues or Queensland Maroons for the 1995 State of Origin series. Sydney Tigers had one representative in the series, with fullback Tim Brasher starting all three games in that position for New South Wales. The war also included controlling rugby league in England and New Zealand. Some say it was a war simply for television broadcasting rights and profiting from the popularity of the sport, yet both the SL and the ARL claimed to have had the best interests of the sport at heart. The SL was reasonably seen by many as the aggressors because they were challenging the incumbent ARL for control in Australia.

As a first year CEO, Danny Munk found himself on the front-
lines, yet how the war impacted Sydney Tigers was surprising. According to Munk,

> Super League probably saved the football club
> in many ways, because suddenly what was hap-
> pening was that the ARL needed to keep the key
> clubs in front…between what the Super League
> was doing funding the clubs that joined the Super
> League…the ARL was changing its funding…the
> grants suddenly increased ten-fold…in '95 and
> '96 Balmain got grants that basically allowed it to
> be financially on the same footing as a number of
> clubs. We were able to use that funding both in
> developing our teams and what we were doing,
> but also growing what the club did. So in many
> ways, strangely enough, without Super League I
> think we would have had a fairly difficult time
> being competitive…because of the Super League
> and ARL war, clubs like us and Souths became
> very competitive. I joined in '95 and the football
> club had a budget of one million dollars…with-
> in two years the budget's four million dollars…
> the money has to come from somewhere…that's
> an exponential growth…during the Super League
> and ARL war sponsors were coming and going
> left, right and centre because they didn't know
> what was going on…Optus were supporting
> the ARL clubs and Telstra supporting the Super
> League clubs…the funding from Optus was the

lifeblood for many [ARL] clubs during that period (Munk 2018).

The 1996 ARL season was a twenty-team premiership, and clubs and players aligned to the SL participated, but the SL made a bold statement by forfeiting the games its clubs were scheduled to play against ARL clubs for Round 1 of the season. The premiership returned to normal by Round 2, but the end result was that twelve teams played twenty-one games and eight played twenty-two for the season. Sydney Tigers took on Sydney City Roosters for Round 1 on March 23 at the Sydney Football Stadium, with the Roosters winning 38–10, and the Tigers were one of the eight teams to play twenty-two games. Sydney Tigers would finish the regular season two wins short of making the top-eight finals, but their record of eleven wins and eleven losses was a positive step forward in terms of performance. They hadn't finished even or greater with wins since 1990, yet their crowd attendance at Leichhardt Oval in 1994, as Balmain Tigers, was still higher, with the average crowd at Parramatta Stadium in 1996 being 5,703 and the highest crowd for the season 10,541. Both were close to 2,000 attendees less than in 1994.

After two seasons of being Sydney Tigers and using Parramatta Stadium as their home venue change fast approached. For Munk it was a straightforward decision: "With Super League happening and for us to be focusing on being part of the ARL…we needed to get back to our grassroots tribalism, and that's when we re-branded back to Balmain Tigers and that's when we also went back to Leichhardt Oval as well" (Munk 2018).

The year 1997 saw two separate competitions, with the SL and the ARL operating concurrently. The SL had ten teams and the ARL had twelve, but interestingly, the remaining five of nine clubs from the 1908 foundation NSWRFL season were all in the ARL, some with slightly different names by 1997, consisting of Sydney City Roosters, South Sydney Rabbitohs, North Sydney Bears, Balmain Tigers, and Western Suburbs Magpies. The SL, though, was more national, with the Adelaide Rams in South Australia and Perth Reds in Western Australia, plus they had an international presence, with the Auckland Warriors in New Zealand. Both leagues were well represented in the traditional rugby league states of New South Wales and Queensland. Even though they were separate leagues, the SL and the ARL combined for twenty-two professional rugby league clubs, and as a result, there were more opportunities for players.

Like a lot of players at Balmain, Adam Nable had begun his playing career elsewhere, and he joined the club for the 1997 season. He was focused and personable, yet his journey to become a Balmain Tiger covered many more kilometres than most. He was a utility player who was comfortable playing either hooker, halfback, or lock, but hooker was his most preferred position. Nable is part of a unique group of rugby league players born in the state of Victoria, where Australian Rules Football is the number-one winter team sport. Rugby league, though, continues to work to increase interest in Victoria, and it has made some progress there since the late 1990s. As he was born in Wodonga, Nable was born almost on the border of rugby league–focused New South Wales. His father, David, was an infantryman in the Royal Australian Army, and the family moved around quite a bit until 1982, when the family settled in Sydney's Northern Beaches. David Nable was a distinguished serviceman, and Adam proudly recalls, "He did a couple of deployments in Borneo and Malaysia. He got himself into the physical training side of the army...he worked his way right up to the top as a Warrant officer class 1...He met Bob Fulton [a rugby league player, then coach] through the army…once he got out of the army completely…he had a fair bit to do with Manly Warringah for about ten or eleven years [physical training, coaching coordinator, and junior development]…he had a fair bit to do there when Manly were going pretty well" (Nable, personal interview, 2018).

In 1982 Adam Nable turned seven years old, and so he grew up on the Northern Beaches and undertook his schooling there. Adam had four siblings, consisting of three brothers and one sister, and sport was a favourite activity for the five Nable children. Adam is the second youngest of the children. Looking back on it, he remembers, "It was pretty competitive…we were always playing footy or boxing or doing something…some of those sparring sessions could get a little bit out of hand…it was always competitive, we were always doing something…When we grew up it was down at the surf club (surf lifesaving club) so we did nippers (junior lifesaving) and that sort of stuff…I didn't really take to another sport apart from footy…I'd go to the footy games, and play footy" (Nable 2018).

The 1980s was an exciting decade for rugby league, and there was no shortage of talent, characters, and quality teams, which in some ways made it difficult to follow just one team. "When I first got to Sydney…I went for Parramatta in the '82 grand final…I loved Manly…I loved Phil Blake and Graham Eadie…Believe it or not I fell in love with the Tigers…I loved that era…Wayne Pearce, Sirro (Paul Sironen), Blocker (Steve Roach), Ellery Hanley…that was my team," said Nable (2018). Interestingly, when Nable joined Balmain in 1997, Hanley and Sironen were both his teammates, and the team was coached by Pearce.

Nable progressed through the lower grades of Manly Warringah. From 1993 to 1995, their first-grade team didn't finish the regular season lower than fourth, and in 1995 they were minor premiers with the best record, but they lost the 1995 grand final. Nable was appreciative and practical when it came to assessing what the club might offer him: "It was a great club...you were right in the mix [with training] there was no divide between first grade and the under twenty-ones...after games everyone was sort of all together...it was a really good culture...I think it was hard because there was a bit of politics there...I felt it was going to be hard for me to get to the top level with what was in front of me...I thought I'm not gonna sort of push it up hill...an opportunity came to go overseas with Wakefield...I was twenty...the money was better at Manly, but I didn't feel there would be any real progression there" (Nable 2018).

Nable made his first-grade debut playing for Manly Warringah during Round 22 on August 27, 1995, when he came off the bench playing at home on Brookvale Oval against South Sydney Rabbitohs. "That team, it was amazing...an Australian [Kangaroo team] front row with Mark Carroll, David Gillespie...unbelievable. You sort of pinch yourself a little bit...It was great," said Nable (2018). Manly Warringah won the game 32–4 and then continued on with their charge all the way to the grand final, but it would be the only first-grade game Nable would play for them.

Adam Nable's second eldest brother, Matthew, appeared in eight first-grade games from 1991 to 1995. Five were with Manly Warringah, from 1991 to 1992, and three for South Sydney, in 1995, and he played his final first-grade game at lock for Souths during Round 13 on June 25, 1995, which meant Adam and Matthew never got to play each other at the first-grade level. As Adam remembers it, "I did play against him (Matthew) when he was at Souths...it was pretty fun...it was a reserve grade game...I laughed...he got super aggressive...[After a tackle] I held him down...he sort of blew up and I just laughed...he was pissed off," (Nable 2018) and Manly Warringah won that game.

After finishing playing rugby league, Matthew put his energy towards boxing; he then became a personal trainer, and he worked as a beer salesman. He then took a bold new direction, drafting a novel that became the screenplay for the rugby league–themed Australian drama film *The Final Winter* (2007). Matthew also starred in the movie. A key part of the narrative includes the brother-versus-brother clash between Mick "Grub" Henderson (played by Matthew) and Trent Henderson, who play on opposing clubs in the NSWRFL of the early 1980s. It's impossible not to wonder what significance Adam and Matthew playing against each other in reserve grade had on the construction of the storyline, or if Matthew playing sports against any of his other brothers played a part, as well. Matthew would find his calling in life as an actor, and another film credit of his includes Mel Gibson's *Hacksaw Ridge* (2016). Matthew has also appeared in many Australian television shows.

Adam's journey to the Balmain Tigers would come via England, and his time abroad included Matthew. "Wakefield-Trinity 1996...It was a great experience...I was twenty...living away from home...It was fantastic...It was good football. Matt played for Carlisle...we were in different divisions...we never played against each other there. I'd signed a contract with Wakefield...it was a two-year deal...it was really pretty minimal sort of money...I'd sort of been getting some offers from clubs over there [England]...there was Wigan, Castleford, and London...Wayne Pearce rang me...my preference was to stay in England, if I could...I came back [to Australia;] Malcolm Reilly contacted me and he wanted me to come to Newcastle...That same day I was going to sit down with Junior Pearce and Danny Munk [about signing with Balmain]...Newcastle Knights fell through for some particular reason…I had to take what Balmain offered me," Nable explained (2018).

While Nable's pathway to Balmain was a bit unsystematic, he was there, and he was part of the club's revival. The last time Balmain played at Leichhardt Oval in 1994 was Round 21 on August 21, against Penrith Panthers. Penrith won the game 22–10, and 7,810 people were in attendance. Gary Freeman had played for Balmain from 1988 to 1991, and that day he was playing halfback for Penrith. Some of his 1989 grand final teammates were playing for Balmain, and Tim Brasher, Michael Neil, Ben Elias, and Steve Edmed played that Sunday in 1994. Players and fans might have reasonably thought that they were there for Balmain's last-ever game at Leichhardt Oval, but 930 days later, they would return there to play Manly Warringah Sea Eagles. The homecoming to Leichhardt Oval was well received by supporters, as 18,247 attended the Round 1 game on March 8, 1997.

Manly Warringah were 1996 minor premiers, and they won the grand final in the twenty-team competition, which included SL-aligned players and clubs. Keeping Manly Warringah in the ARL was a massive positive, because they were without a doubt the best club in 1996, which deprived the SL of some marketing superiority. Manly Warringah had retained much of their 1996 first-grade player roster, and Balmain had quite a task in front of them, facing Manly Warringah as their first opponent for the 1997 season. The game would also be Adam Nable's debut for Balmain, as he came off the bench, and playing against his former club had some significance, too. "It was fantastic…it was an amazing experience to play at Leichhardt Oval…it was an intense game…every time we played against Manly we always played well against them," said Nable (2018). Manly Warringah won the game 14–10, but Balmain played a competitive game, and despite the loss, it was a solid effort for them to push such a fancied club—Manly Warringah would be the ARL's minor premiers and grand finalists in 1997.

Balmain would lose their first three games of the 1997 season, but their maiden victory came against South Sydney Rabbitohs in Round 4 on March 30 at Leichhardt Oval, winning 22–16. By Round 8, Balmain had won four and lost four games, and with the top seven teams earning finals berths in the ARL twelve-club competition, they were in with a chance. Injury caused Nable to miss Rounds 4 to 11, and he found himself lining up against Manly Warringah again for Round 12, but this time at their home, Brookvale Oval. Having spent so much time there as a junior player and then as a graded player, he still felt it had a sense of home to it. He was named on the bench, and wins for Balmain at Brookvale had been very scarce. Their last was Round 16 on June 16, 1984, with Balmain winning 15–4. Interestingly, Balmain was coached by Frank Stanton from 1981 to 1986, and prior to that, Stanton had coached Manly Warringah from 1975 to 1979. His resume also included coaching the New South Wales Blues and Australia. The 1984 win at Brookvale, though, became elusive to replicate, despite some close games played there, and they split the points for their Round 21 game on August 19, 1989, with a 10–10 draw.

In 1997, on paper, Manly Warringah was the far superior team, and Balmain venturing to Brookvale for Round 12 on May 31 would be seen by some as a certain victory for Manly Warringah. Balmain was also hoping to snap a three-game losing streak, and one more loss would make it Balmain's longest slide of the season. The game had some sting to it, and when a scuffle broke out close to the halfway line, Balmain didn't take a backwards step. They took on whatever challenge was put to them, and when it was all over,

Balmain won 14–10, which, interestingly, was the reverse score of their Round 1 game.

From 1997 to 1999, as a Balmain Tiger, Nable played against Manly Warringah six times, and Balmain during those years had an even record with them, with three wins and three losses. Considering the high calibre of the Manly Warringah clubs during those years, it was a good record. Balmain seemed to find a way to step it up for them. For Nable the games had some consistent points: "They were always physical games…they [Manly Warringah] were always that benchmark" (Nable 2018). Three times during the 1997 season, Balmain had back-to-back wins, in Rounds 4–5, 7–8, and 12–13. Their results kept them close to the top seven, but for the most part they sat in eighth or ninth place on the ladder. Their last four games, Rounds 19–22, would be crucial to gaining a spot in the top seven for the finals. They could guarantee it with three wins, and even with two wins, if results went their way, they could still sneak in. Some might say finishing sixth or seventh would only lead to a quick exit from the finals, but for a club that hadn't reached the finals since 1990, it would be an achievement.

Balmain's Round 19 game was on August 10 against South Queensland Crushers at Leichhardt Oval, and Balmain's 32–14 win was a solid team effort and kept their season momentum in good order. For Nable the game had some personal significance: "John Jones, [front row/second rower] he played at Manly and he was on the backend of his career [playing for South Queensland Crushers]…I think he came out of the line and a hole opened up…I just went and scored…he came up to me after the game and said, 'I went past him like he was standing still, and maybe it's time for me [Jones] to hang up the boots,'" said Nable (2018) with a respectful laugh. It was Nable's first career try as a first-grade player, and since

Round 15 he had been starting at halfback.

Nable's versatility and ability to defend helped complement a Balmain club that few gave much of a chance at the beginning of the 1997 season. Sydney City Roosters defeated Balmain 18–10 during Round 20, and while it was a competitive result against a classy team, the pressure was on Balmain to win. It didn't get any easier, because for Round 21 they faced high-flying Parramatta Eels at Leichhardt Oval on August 22. It was a Friday night, and with 18,203 people in attendance, the place was packed out, and Balmain badly needed the win. Few would have predicted Balmain winning 26–6, and no one that watched the game could possibly forget thirty-six-year-old Englishman Ellery Hanley's swoop on a slightly wayward Parramatta pass, intercepting the ball against the run of play, and him scurrying nearly from the halfway mark of the field for his final career try. It was Hanley's last game at Leichhardt Oval, and it was a brilliant win for the club. In 1988 he joined Balmain for the final three games of the regular season, and many are satisfied that his spark as a player contributed to Balmain winning six games in a row, which included four finals games, taking the club all the way to the 1988 grand final.

Newcastle Knights were red hot in 1997, and Balmain's Round 22 game would be played at Marathon Stadium in Newcastle. If Balmain won the game, they would be certain to secure a top-seven finish and qualify for the finals, but Newcastle won 34–10. A finals berth wasn't to be, with the Gold Coast Charges wrapping up the seventh spot on the ladder. They had the same number of wins as Balmain, but they had one draw, which meant they had one fewer loss than Balmain. It was also bittersweet, considering that Balmain lost both of their season games to Gold Coast, which included playing them at home during Round 14, where Gold Coast won 22–20.

Even though they didn't make the 1997 finals, Balmain had proven to be better than many experts predicted, with some expecting them to finish in last place that year.

The year 1998 brought with it wonderful peace, as the SL and ARL war had come to an end and the game was united under the National Rugby League (NRL). The war had its casualties, with SL clubs Hunter Mariners and Perth Reds and the ARL's South Queensland Crushers departed. It can reasonably be argued, though, that both Perth and South Queensland were financially incapable of going much further anyway, and Newcastle could sustain only one team, making Hunter the odd one out. The year 1998 would see a twenty-team premiership and the first year of the Melbourne Storm. It was easy enough for fans and clubs to assume the war was over and that peace would be everlasting, yet the NRL made no secret of the fact that there would need to be a further reduction of the number of clubs.

The idea of merging Balmain with another club had been mentioned prior to 1998, but the talk got louder that year. As Balmain's CEO, Danny Munk, recalls,

> The board wanted to investigate all options…
> as a board you can't be close minded to things…
> there were invitations from Norths and we had a
> conversation…we had conversations with Souths,
> but that one didn't go very far because Souths were
> adamant that there was going to be no amalgamation with anybody and they were going to stand
> alone…We got an approach from the guys at the
> Sharks…there was a chat but that didn't go too
> far…there were even conversations with Easts…
> with Norths there was a number of chats around

that…and in some cases it was both boards just making sure they asked the question [of possibly merging together] because the management of the board has a responsibility to do that…and certainly we were encouraged by the ARL [and NRL] to have conversations with Parramatta…and those conversations certainly showed there was a lot of good synergies between Parramatta and Balmain…and certainly the fact we shared [territory] borders with the inner-west and west…both licensed venues were growing…a lot of things made sense (Munk 2018).

The media flung around ideas and rumours, and one was the idea of merging Balmain with Gold Coast and becoming the East Coast Tigers based out of southeast Queensland. A number of other Sydney clubs were mentioned along the way, yet the talk of merging Balmain faded a bit into the background when they won five of their first six games of the 1998 season. In Rounds 3–6 they won four games in a row, and suddenly a Balmain renaissance surprised many experts, but losing four in a row in Rounds 7–10 cooled things down a bit. During the second half of the season, in Rounds 13–24, Balmain won three games and lost eight. Their Round 20 game against the Brisbane Broncos at Leichhardt Oval on July 25 was special in its own way, as Brisbane were having a strong season, and they would go on to win the 1998 minor premiership and grand final. That Saturday night they met a determined Balmain, and the 10–10 draw could be considered a victory against an opponent who on paper was far superior. The season ended with four consecutive losses, which took some of the spark out of what was a notably competitive season by Balmain.

Front rower Paul Sironen was the last player left at the club who had appeared in either the 1988 or 1989 grand final [he played in both], and he had announced that 1998 would be his final season. His first-grade debut for Balmain was during Round 18 on July 7, 1985, against the Canterbury-Bankstown Bulldogs at their home venue, Belmore Sports Ground. Sironen came off the bench in jersey number 26, and Balmain won the game 18–12. He played his entire career as a Tiger, and with Balmain having no chance of making the finals, Round 24 on August 22 would be Sironen's farewell at Leichhardt Oval against the Sydney City Roosters. That Saturday night the Roosters no doubt had respectful feelings for Sironen and his career, but business was business, and they were a strong team bound for the finals. The Roosters won 40–4. Sironen was given the ball to convert Balmain's lone try, scored by second rower Mark O'Neill, but the kick was to be taken somewhat to the right of the goal posts, and Sironen wasn't able to boot it through. It was nevertheless an honourable gesture to have him attempt converting the try.

Adam Nable played lock that game and said of it, "I remember watching those [Balmain Tigers] grand finals [1988 and 1989] as a kid...to be there in that environment [with retired players from that era watching on and Sironen playing his final game for Balmain]...It was an honour...He was just such a leader...He'd pick the ball up and do everything...How do you replace that? Everybody looked up to him...When he left that hole was huge to fill... To top that off he was just such a good bloke...I remember vividly as a kid when the Tigers played Manly in the '86 [minor-preliminary] qualifying-final he [Sironen] just tore them to pieces" (Nable 2018). The day Nable spoke of was Saturday, September 6, and Balmain won the game 29–22. Sironen contributed to the points with a try, which happened to be the first of his career, in front of 17,597 people at the Sydney Cricket Ground.

Balmain finishing the 1998 season thirteenth of twenty teams was proof of some competitiveness and well ahead of the experts' early predictions for them, which was close to the bottom of the premiership. The top ten teams qualified for the finals that year. The Gold Coast Charges and Adelaide Rams were culled from the NRL for the 1999 season, and the St. George Dragons and Illawarra Steelers merged, becoming St. George Illawarra Dragons. St. George Illawarra would be a key case study for the possibility of merges. Improving on their 1998 season was a reasonable goal for Balmain, yet the effects of losing some quality players to other clubs after 1996 and 1997 became more visible by 1998, and by 1999 assessing some of the departed players was frustratingly thought-provoking. Retirements ensured that no other clubs got the benefit of players in that situation, but players moving to other clubs sometimes had a way of reminding Balmain of these players' talents and the impact it could have on their old club. Plus, plenty of Balmain Tigers fans would quickly miss them and especially feel the loss when they wore the uniform of another team.

## CHAPTER 2

# LOSING SOME TALENTED TIGERS

Front rower Corey Pearson was a local guy when it came to Balmain's traditional catchment area, as a graduate of nearby Drummoyne Boys' High School. He made his first-grade debut off the bench as a Sydney Tiger during Round 12 on Saturday, June 17, 1995, at their then home, Parramatta Stadium, playing against the South Queensland Crushers. The Tigers won the game 16–12, and from South Queensland's inaugural season from 1995 to their final season in 1997, they met four times, and Sydney/Balmain Tigers won each game. Pearson scored his first career try as a Sydney Tiger during Round 15 on Saturday, July 13, 1996, at Belmore Sports Ground against the Canterbury-Bankstown Bulldogs. Sydney Tigers won the game 20–18, and Pearson started the game as a front rower. For ten minutes, second rower Darren Senter was in the sin bin, and the fact that the Tigers won despite having to play with twelve men on thirteen for those minutes was a credit to the effort of the whole team.

In 1996 Pearson was just twenty-three years old and still had a lot of good football ahead of him. The fan rumour mill always has its share of truth and fiction, but it was said Pearson and Coach Wayne Pearce didn't agree on everything. Pearson has a careful diplomacy about him, and even if he is asked a loaded question, he will respond by saying something like, "I know what you mean, but I can't comment on that." Pearson's departure didn't play out with any particularly ugly slanging matches by proxy through the media; Pearson instinctively knew better than that. Pearson played his last game as a Sydney Tiger during Round 22 on Sunday, September 1, 1996. They played Sydney City Roosters at Parramatta Stadium that day, and Sydney City won the game 24–10.

Pearson joined St. George Dragons for the 1997 season, and during Round 6 on April 13, 1997, he faced his old club at his new home, Kogarah Oval. He came off the bench that game, and St. George won 16–10, but a try not awarded to Balmain Tigers centre William Kennedy, which might have locked the game up with a converted goal, was probably one of the worst refereeing decisions of the entire 1997 ARL season. It was deemed that Kennedy did not properly ground the ball over the line, but based on video replay, many looking on thought very differently about that decision. Pearson had nevertheless participated in a win over his old club, but Balmain got one back by defeating St. George during Round 17 on Saturday, July 26, at Leichhardt Oval, winning 10–4. Pearson started the game as a front rower, and some might have thought Balmain was doing fairly well without him, but 1998 would be the year fans of rugby league would see Pearson in full throttle.

From the start of the 1998 season, he was one of the form front rowers, with punishing runs at defensive lines, plus he had some finer skills in terms of a short passing game that speedy outside backs could run off, and he could kick the ball with some purpose if the situation called for it. Balmain and St. George met at Kogarah

Oval during Round 12 on Saturday, May 30, 1998, and St. George won the game 28–2, which included a try by Pearson. As it became apparent that 1998 would be Balmain front rower Paul Sironen's final season, it was impossible for anyone watching on to not at least briefly ponder the value Pearson could have added to Balmain.

With the amalgamation of the St. George Dragons and Illawarra Steelers, the new club was spoiled for choice when it came to front rowers [Andrew Hart, Chris Leikvoll, Craig Smith, Colin Ward, and Pearson] for their inaugural 1999 season. Pearson for the majority of the season started games as a front rower. St. George Illawarra Dragons would go on to play in the 1999 grand final. Pearson unfortunately missed the game due to injury, but he was a notable go-forward man in the rampaging juggernaut that was the 1999 St. George Illawarra club.

When Sironen retired in 1998, Balmain knew they had a task on their hands to find a player who could offer output close to Sironen's, and they would in fact recruit a good front rower for 1999 (Jason Lowrie), yet it was becoming more apparent as the 1999 season neared for Balmain that they would need player depth to be able to compete with the more fancied clubs. Pearson was still only twenty-six years old in 1999 and in the prime of his career. There was absolutely no doubt he would have complemented the team well, and with Lowrie, Pearson, and Shane Walker, this would have ensured that Balmain wasn't stretched thin and had experienced and highly competent front rowers. It would have also allowed the three to be rotated, with one coming off the bench, which might have helped better share the workload and added extra grunt to Balmain's forward pack. Alas, Pearson was gone, but his ability was hard to forget.

Lock forward Glenn Morrison made his first-grade debut as

a Sydney Tiger during Round 1 on Saturday, March 23, 1996, at the Sydney Football Stadium against Sydney City Roosters. He came off the bench that game, and Sydney City won 38–10, but by Round 4 Morrison made his first start at lock, and he started in that position nearly every game of the 1996 season. In Round 4, Sydney Tigers played the Newcastle Knights on Sunday, April 14, 1996, at Newcastle's Marathon Stadium, and the Tigers won the game 24–12. There was some personal significance in this game for Morrison, because he had grown up slightly south of there on the New South Wales Central Coast, and he scored his maiden first-grade try that game, which contributed to a solid win by the Tigers.

Morrison impressed at lock, and he would go on to be awarded Dally M Rookie of the Year for the 1996 season. Some people were saying he was the best lock the club had had since Wayne Pearce, and having turned twenty years old on May 28, 1996, he was predicted to have a big future ahead of him. By 1997 rumours circulated that Morrison was leaving Balmain at the end of the season to join the North Sydney Bears. In 1997 he would earn an NSW Country jersey, and on Friday, April 25, he would come off the bench during Country's 17–4 win over NSW City.

Morrison had an impressive 1997 season with the Balmain Tigers, appearing in twenty club games and earning his first representative jersey, but he was joining North Sydney for 1998. Morrison was quoted most by the media as saying his decision to leave was heavily based on the uncertainty of Balmain's future as a club. Even then (in 1997), there was some irony to his decision to sign with North Sydney, because they were far from completely stable and secure. As time went on, they were planning to relocate to Gosford on the Central Coast in a bid to better their own situation and hopefully secure their long-term future. Not much was said, though, about North Sydney's mounting debt. By 1999 North Sydney's financial difficulties were much more apparent, and 1999 would have even more irony for Morrison, given his reported concerns about the future of Balmain.

Yet back in 1997, few Balmain fans were convinced Morrison was leaving solely because of club uncertainty. It was rumoured that Morrison had signed a lucrative deal with North Sydney and that Balmain were not in a position to match or better the offer. What scratched the skin of some Balmain faithful was the view that Morrison hadn't been at Balmain long (two seasons in first grade, 1996–1997), and he wasn't respecting the time, effort, and opportunity the club had given him. From their point of view, it looked like Morrison had used Balmain for all he could, and he was leaving for big money at the first chance he got. There are some unwritten rules or even an expectation in sport that players owe something to their club, especially if it is considered that the club stimulated or helped cultivate or better a player's career. Rightfully or wrongfully, some Balmain fans took the view that Morrison was ungrateful and disrespectful to the club by signing with North Sydney.

It also didn't help that Morrison's uncertain future at Balmain played itself out somewhat in the media in 1997, and it seemed to drag through too much of the season. In fairness to Morrison, his perspective needed to be considered, and joining North Sydney would potentially become a homecoming for him to the NSW Central Coast. He would be joining a club that had played in the finals in 1991 and each season from 1994 to 1997, and if the rumours were true, he'd be making a lot more money playing for them.

Morrison made forty-one first-grade appearances playing for the Tigers from 1996 to 1997. His final game was Round 22 on August 30, 1997, at Newcastle's Marathon Stadium—that final regular-season game Balmain needed to win to secure a 1997 finals spot, but which Newcastle won 34–10. There was no formal farewell for Morrison; it wasn't like he was retiring or had played one hundred or more games for the club. He was leaving a club where he had earned the position of lock—and it could have been his for possibly a long time—to join North Sydney, whose incumbent lock was the inspiring Billy Moore, who had represented Australia and Queensland.

Morrison could play second row, but North Sydney was stacked with Adam Muir (newly recruited for 1998) and long-serving David Fairleigh, both of whom had played for Australia and New South Wales. So with the exception of injuries, Morrison would be coming off the bench for North Sydney, and for the most part, that's exactly how it played out for him in 1998, as he only started six of the twenty-two games he appeared in. To add to the challenge, North Sydney also had Willie Leyshon, and he was a second rower or lock. In 1998 he had a breakthrough year, appearing in a career-high twenty-four games. Leyshon was born the same year as Morrison (1976), and Balmain fans couldn't help but shake their heads as Morrison played behind so many other players in 1998.

Morrison would face his old club once in 1998, during Round 22, when North Sydney played Balmain at North Sydney Oval on Saturday, August 8, and he came off the bench. North Sydney won 22–6, and Morrison scored a try against his old club. Morrison got to experience finals play with North Sydney, as the club finished fifth, earning a top-ten qualifying spot, but the club lost both their finals games. In 1999 Morrison would play against Balmain twice, and during Round 6 on April 10 at Leichhardt Oval, he came off the bench, with North Sydney winning 26–4. The clubs met again during Round 13 on May 30 at North Sydney Oval. Morrison started at lock, and North Sydney romped to victory at 64–12. He scored two tries that game, but North Sydney would finish the 1999 season fourteenth of seventeen teams, with just eight wins and sixteen losses.

North Sydney was reportedly four million dollars in debt at that time, as well. Their plan to relocate to Gosford didn't save them, and they would find themselves in an uncomfortable merger with Manly Warringah, becoming the Northern Eagles, from 2000 to 2002. Home games were shared between Brookvale Oval and NorthPower Stadium. By 2003, they were demerged, with Manly Warringah the sole entity.

Morrison never got his Central Coast homecoming, because he joined the North Queensland Cowboys for the 2000 season. He would play for NSW Country again in 2001 and 2003–2005, but his representative career never progressed beyond that. Some like to say that if he had stayed at Balmain, he would have played for the New South Wales Blues and possibly Australia, and just maybe the continuity of a career as a Tiger might have helped him get there. He appeared in 222 first-grade games and another 102 in the English Super League, accumulating a massive career, but there were those who wanted him to do it all as a Tiger. North Sydney's demise was ironic, considering that Morrison was adamant in 1997 that Balmain's future was so uncertain then, but Balmain recruited Ben Duckworth from the Sydney City Roosters for the 1998 season, and he took over playing lock for Balmain. Duckworth was undervalued at his former clubs, and at Balmain he showcased his talents, but he didn't have the same durability as Morrison.

It's interesting how something is said or written, and despite the information not being correct, it easily becomes accepted fact, as happened to talented backline player Tim Brasher a few times during his career. Brasher has gone down in Balmain Tigers folklore as a seventeen-year-old centre that broke into first grade while still in high school in 1989. This has been said by fans and teammates, but he was born on March 16, 1971, and had already turned eighteen before Balmain's season started on March 18. Brasher made his first-grade debut for Balmain during Round 5 on April 16 at Orana Park against the Western Suburbs Magpies, and he came off the bench during the game, which Western Suburbs won 6–4.

Another misreported detail of Brasher's career was him making his first-grade debut against the Penrith Panthers at Penrith Park, but the game against Penrith was actually his second first-grade appearance, during Round 7 on April 29, 1989. Penrith won the game 28–8, and Brasher came off the bench for Balmain. Brasher's maiden first-grade try was scored during Round 12 on Saturday, June 17, at Leichhardt Oval against South Sydney Rabbitohs. It was the only try scored by Balmain that day, as South Sydney went on to win 10–8. It was also Brasher's third first-grade career start as a centre.

It was nevertheless an incredible first season for him, as he appeared in twenty first-grade games, which included Balmain's charge all the way to the 1989 grand final. During that first season, he established himself as a centre, and through to 1992 he would mix his time in the backline also, as a winger, fullback, and five-eighth. Brilliant and incumbent Balmain fullback Garry Jack retired after the 1992 season, which opened up the fullback position, and Brasher comfortably made it his own.

By 1992, Brasher had debuted for the NSW Blues, and from 1993 to 1998, he was first choice at fullback for the Blues. He had also represented Australia at World Cups and other international matches. Considering the struggles for consistent form by Balmain/

Sydney Tigers from 1991 to 1996, Brasher still excelled. His skills certainly caught the attention of other clubs, but Brasher stayed when others might have moved on. Teammate Paul Sironen had seen Brasher's journey from the beginning, and Sironen made special mention of it in his autobiography, *Sirro! Tales from Tiger Town:*

> When I read about Timmy [Brasher] being offered $700,000 to join Penrith last year [1996] I couldn't help but chuckle at my memory of when he joined the Tigers as a schoolboy, because the little bugger never had any money. During the semi-finals in '89 we'd go swimming every Thursday night and then, as part of our preparation, the entire team would have a meal at a restaurant. We gorged ourselves for $25 a head. Well, that kind of cash was beyond Timmy's reach back then so we'd chip in to buy the young fella a feed. I laugh at that memory nowadays because Tim could buy the joint out if he wanted to. I made Brash see red last year when the newspaper broke the news of his deal with Penrith, because it coincided with our match against Norths in which he missed some telling tackles. They definitely didn't help our cause and after the game I said, 'Brash, you've been offered $690,000 for your attack and $10,000 for your defence.' And boy, it went down badly. Despite my tongue-in-cheek barb, I rate Tim as one of the game's elite players (Sironen with Lane 1997, p. 124).

By 1997, talk about whether Brasher would stay at Balmain played out a bit in the media, which wasn't helped by his uncertain replies. One popular fan-fuelled story goes that Brasher was set to re-sign with Balmain, but he reportedly arrived fifteen minutes late to the meeting, and the offer was pulled. For some fans, this abrupt ending became lore, but Brasher was a veteran of 185 first-grade appearances as a Tiger, and frankly, these fans should have known a lot better. Balmain's CEO Danny Munk sheds some real light on what happened:

> The whole Tim Brasher negotiation had gone on for a very long time…it got to a point where decisions were made…the whole negotiation had been going on for months and months…offers had been put on the table…and they were significant offers and they could have been accepted at any time…so the fact that it got to a point when a deadline was issued highlighted the frustration for the club…By the time Tim decided there were no other offers out there that he was happy with, the club had gotten to the point where it decided 'If we're not your first choice then we're not your choice at all'…the thing with the deadlines was that it was not said it's in five minutes time… there were communications with his agent going 'we need an answer in two weeks' time, we need an answer in a weeks' time, what's going on this has been on the table a long time?'…at the end of the day in most cases you deal with the [player's] agent…if you put a deadline and it doesn't happen…there's a point where you've just got to say, 'There's that much money on the table, if that's not good enough, then we've got to go

elsewhere'…I have to say, was there any satisfaction in the fact that Tim went elsewhere? No. I think both parties, the Tigers and Tim, probably would have preferred with hindsight that it ended up differently. I think Tim is still very loyal to the Tigers…he was a big part of the Tigers during the late eighties and nineties…he was someone that the Tigers wanted to have long-term…Tim still has to this day a relationship with the Tigers…The fact that a contract didn't get re-signed in the end didn't mean the relationship ended…Tim Brasher is one highly intelligent individual (Munk 2018).

The 1997 season would be Brasher's last as a Balmain Tiger, but unlike Morrison, there was no one club that Brasher was reportedly in formal or informal agreement with. As it would turn out, that Round 22 game in Newcastle that Balmain needed to win had even more significance, as it was also Brasher's final game as a Tiger. Saturday, August 30, 1997, and Newcastle's 34–10 win had layers both seen and unseen at the time. Losing the game meant Balmain lost the opportunity to guarantee a finals berth, that was clear, but the impact of losing Morrison and Brasher to other clubs wasn't necessarily fully digested at the time by fans. There was always that bit of hope that there was still time for them to decide to stay with Balmain, but as the rest of 1997 progressed, so did the certainty that both players were gone forever. Considering that Brasher had made close to 200 first-grade appearances for Balmain, it was unfortunate there was no opportunity to farewell him on the field in 1997.

For 1998, Brasher signed with the South Sydney Rabbitohs, and when it became public, it was difficult for some Balmain fans to accept that Brasher was leaving to join a club that had finished well behind eighth-placed Balmain, as South Sydney finished eleventh of twelve teams in 1997. Further to this, Balmain's thirteenth-place finish in 1998 was ahead of South Sydney's eighteenth of twenty teams that season. Brasher had another year at South Sydney before joining the North Queensland Cowboys in 2000, which somewhat ironically found him back on a club with Glenn Morrison.

For 1998, Balmain recruited Manly Warringah fullback Shannon Nevin, and all twenty appearances Nevin made for Balmain in 1998 were at fullback. Nevin took the opportunity with enthusiasm, having had to often play behind other players for much of his first-grade career at Manly Warringah from 1995 to 1997, with twenty-nine appearances during that time, but trying to replace a player of Brasher's calibre and history at Balmain was challenging.

The impact of the departures of Pearson, Morrison, and Brasher to other clubs wasn't necessarily immediately apparent, but this was partially due to Balmain thereafter remaining quite competitive with existing and newly acquired personnel. Balmain had its share of highlights and some notable disappointments during the 1997 and 1998 seasons, but the reduction from twenty teams in 1998 to seventeen in 1999 meant that for a second consecutive year, clubs had an opportunity to strengthen their teams, but this time with players from two ceased clubs (the Adelaide Rams and Gold Coast Charges) and the merger of two clubs (the St. George Dragons and Illawarra Steelers).

In 1998, new club Melbourne Storm finished third of twenty teams during their inaugural season, and they had plucked plenty of talent from two of the defunct clubs. Just to name some of the players, from the Western Reds, they picked up Matt Geyer, Rodney Howe, and Robbie Kearns. From Hunter Mariners, Brett Kimmorley, Robbie Ross, and Richard Swain, and this group of players had either already played for New South Wales or Australia or were incumbent players on those teams or would play at one or more of those levels in the near future. In the case of Swain, he played for New Zealand. So for 1999, the scramble was on for Balmain to recruit as well as possible, but it didn't necessarily mean trying to get as many representative players as Melbourne had in total (they had also recruited from a number of other clubs for 1998); rather, it was about accumulating the best possible quality player depth so Balmain could continue with their competitiveness. Balmain had pushed on despite losing some talent to other clubs during previous years, yet its recruitment for 1999 would be amongst its most active and audacious of the decade. There would be new faces, but there would also be a terrible tragedy.

# CHAPTER 3

# TEAM TRAGEDY

Mata'itai Savaii Savea was a twenty-year-old centre who signed with the Balmain Tigers for the 1999 season and was known by the shortened version of his name, Tai Savea. Savea grew up in suburban Auckland, New Zealand. He rose quickly through the junior ranks, and in 1997 he was selected as a Junior Kiwi, which at the time was a junior national rugby league team consisting of the best players aged eighteen years old or younger, and they would play teams like the Australian School Boys. In 1997 he played under-19s for the Auckland Warriors, and they finished the season as minor premiers playing in the Super League competition, as well as reaching the under-19 grand final. As an under-19s player, Savea was "an engaging character—happy, outgoing, great to coach, and a great teammate. He was an explosive ball runner who ran terrific centre lines—had a deceptive left foot step a la [Brad] Fittler—big and strong," said his under-19s coach, John Ackland (personal interview, 2018). In 1998 he played reserve grade for the Auckland Warriors before crossing the Tasman Sea to join Balmain for 1999.

"Tai was recommended to us [the Balmain Tigers] by a scout

over in New Zealand...we started training in early November [1998] that offseason...he impressed at training, his attitude was great...he was a fairly quietly spoken guy...[Savea was] quite solidly built, he certainly had the frame to be a good player, had the skills to be a good NRL player," said Balmain first-grade coach Wayne Pearce (personal interview, 2018).

"I trained with him for a couple of weeks and he was a popular young Kiwi kid...there was a lot of wraps on him...he was a quiet sort of guy...I was a new kid [new to the club], he was a new kid," said Balmain teammate Joel Caine (personal interview, 2018).

"My memories are of a fresh-faced kid who was excited to know that in the next twelve months he had an opportunity to play with a major rugby league team...this was a kid who had amazing talent...'99 we didn't have a bad team, we had a number of guys who were older, and so for a young person it was a great opportunity," said Balmain Tigers CEO Danny Munk (2018).

For anyone that knew Savea, his trademark was a beaming smile and a very good nature. He caught the attention of astute Balmain Tigers fans as the club described him as a robust centre when confirming news of his signing in late 1998. The club had signed other players with first-grade experience as centres, but most people who followed rugby league closely knew Auckland Warriors had a lot of talent in their lower grades, and it helped that they had a whole country to draw their players from.

Sadly, Savea drowned on December 31, 1998. Munk recalls the news of Savea's death: "That phone call shocked everyone... when teams have a break leading into the Christmas period no one expects everyone not to come back...it had a huge impact on everybody...any loss like that has a massive impact...that's why as a team and organisation you act as if it's a family event, it's like losing a family member because the impact is the same…that's why Wayne Pearce and others went over there [to New Zealand]…something like that happens, it impacts everybody" (Munk 2018).

During the six to eight weeks Savea was at Balmain in late 1998, Pearce had nearly daily interaction with him at training and for related preparations for the season ahead. Pearce remembers,

> We were all due back for training during the early days of January…I got a quite devastating phone call during the break, which was a massive shock, that he had drowned over there in New Zealand…that was something that was really hard to comprehend because he was such a ball of energy…I went over to New Zealand to represent the club at the funeral, I said a few words at the service, and then came back and we resumed training because word had gotten around to a lot of the players, there was an article in the newspaper, so we got everybody together and explained the situation, what had happened to him…we had a memorial service for him, which was quite moving and emotional…it was a very traumatic period dealing with the loss of someone, who everyone got to like and got close to…[As a player] he had a good step, a good turn of speed, and he was quite strong…he was someone I had high hope for because he certainly showed during that couple of months before Christmas that he had a ton of ability…it was tragic that he didn't get the opportunity to show what he could do [at NRL level] (Pearce 2018).

News broke publicly during the early days of January 1999. A *New Zealand Herald* story by Richard Knight titled "Promising League Player and Mate Perish Fishing" reported:

> Tai Savea had two loves in his life, his faith in God and his rugby league.
>
> It was faith in God that kept his family strong while they searched for his body and that of his fishing companion Billy Roebeck at Port Waikato yesterday.
>
> Police divers joined the search in the afternoon and recovered Mr Savea's body last night.
>
> Mr Roebeck, aged 17, from Manurewa in Manukau City, and Mr Savea, 20, were fishing with a church group.
>
> Constable Dan Borrell said they, and two other men, had been up to their necks in water as they dragged a net for mullet near a rocky outcrop about 3km upstream from the Waikato River mouth.
>
> The area is renowned for deep and dangerous holes and Constable Borrell said it was thought one of the men initially stepped into a hole and disappeared.
>
> "There were four of them on a drag net and they were walking it through the water.
>
> "The one right at the deep end got into difficulties and the next one in went to help him and they both disappeared at the same spot," he said.
>
> Mr Savea's father, Tema, said he was told of the tragedy when he returned home from attend-

ing a New Year function at church.

"I couldn't believe it. Tai told me earlier that he was going fishing but promised he would not be late for church that evening.

"He was supposed to fly to Sydney on Sunday to start training for his new rugby league club, Balmain."

Savea was a former Junior Kiwi who recently signed with Balmain and played for the Auckland Warriors.

Kiwi coach Frank Endacott said Savea was a promising player and was destined to play first-grade football.

Savea returned to the country to spend time with his family and attend a friend's wedding.

There was also a subsequent story in the *New Zealand Herald* from early January 1999 titled "Heroic Action Cost Life," which provided some further information:

PORT WAIKATO - Police have hailed as a hero a South Auckland youth who died while trying to save rising rugby league player Tai Savea from drowning at Port Waikato last week.

The body of 17-year-old Billy Roebeck, of Manurewa, was found floating in the Waikato River on Saturday afternoon.

The body of Mr Savea, a 20-year-old former Junior Kiwi and new Balmain Tigers player, had been found by police divers the day before.

The pair drowned on Thursday while net-fishing for mullet from a rocky outcrop about 3km from the river mouth.

Constable Dean Borrell said Mr Roebeck went to help Mr Savea, a non-swimmer, when he stepped into a hole.

"He tried to get him into a lifesaving position, but could not," Constable Borrell said. "His actions were heroic. He lost his own life trying to save somebody else."

Members of Mr Roebeck's family and friends, about 40 people in all, were at Port Waikato when his body was found about 1 pm.

A family service will be held on Friday, followed by burial the next day.

A service for Mr Savea will be held on Wednesday, again with burial the next day.

It was a terrible tragedy, and for it to occur at a time when people celebrate the arrival of a new year would forever change that time of the year for the family and friends of Savea and Roebeck. Even though Savea had not yet played for Balmain, his passing struck at the hearts of the club and its supporters. In Auckland, Savea has been honoured with the Tai Savea Memorial Shield, which is an annual multisport tournament between Henderson Intermediate and Kedgley Intermediate Schools (Savea had attended both of those schools).

Losing a teammate was a very unfortunate start to Balmain's preparation for the 1999 season, and there is no doubt Savea would have complemented the club, with all his skills and admirable demeanour. The club had recruited extensively, however, so there were a lot of new faces at Balmain for the 1999 season.

## CHAPTER 4

# BALMAIN'S NEW RECRUITS FOR 1999

Amongst Balmain's 1999 new recruits, there were thirteen players that had prior first-grade experience at other clubs, and they would all appear for Balmain during the season. These consisted of Joel Caine, John Carlaw, Craig Field, Craig Hancock, Solomon Haumono, Jason Lowrie, Michael Ostini, Steven Price, Nick Shaw, Brad Smith, Tyran Smith, Garth Wood, and Justin Yeo. The club had also recruited a number of young players from other clubs that would make their first-grade debuts as Balmain Tigers in 1999.

With the retirement of club great Paul Sironen at the end of the 1998 season, finding a front rower with experience that could add further spark and impact to Balmain's forward pack was seen to early enough that the new signee was able to attend Sironen's official farewell party in 1998. Jason Lowrie had made 105 first-grade appearances for Eastern Suburbs/Sydney City Roosters from 1993 to 1998, and he had made his first-grade debut for Eastern Suburbs during Round 1 on Sunday, March 14, 1993, at Marathon Stadium, coming off the bench in a game against the Newcastle

Knights, which Eastern Suburbs won 20–10. He had played for New Zealand at different times since 1993 and would also do so in 1999. Due to injury, he only appeared in five first-grade games for Sydney City in 1998, but Balmain was unperturbed and promptly signed him.

Lowrie had a bit of a monkey on his back, which he comfortably laughed about during his career, as he had appeared in over one hundred first-grade games but hadn't scored a try. That would change in 1999, but not while playing for Balmain. After the season ended, Lowrie played for New Zealand in the Tri-Nations, and on Friday, October 15, at Ericsson Stadium, playing against Australia, he scored a try for New Zealand, and New Zealand won the game 24–22. He would score another try at international level later that month, but it would take until April 8, 2000, for him to score a try in the NRL. Lowrie's role at Balmain wasn't about being a prolific try scorer, though; he was a major piece to contribute to Balmain's go-forward and to doggedly defend.

Second rower Solomon Haumono was another brilliant signing. At twenty-three years old, he had already appeared in 64 first-grade games. Interestingly, he had made his first-grade debut for Manly Warringah during Round 11 on Saturday, May 28, 1994, against the Balmain Tigers at Leichhardt Oval. Haumono came off the bench for Manly Warringah, and they won that game 42–0.

He joined the Canterbury-Bankstown Bulldogs in 1997, but 1998 would be an unfortunate year for him, as he walked out on the club while their season was under way to visit a purported girl-friend in England. Gabrielle "The Pleasure Machine" Richens, a little-known British model and actress, was supposedly Haumono's love interest, and having met her in Sydney and become besotted by her, he had gone in pursuit of her to England. The situation suddenly lifted Richens's profile in Australia, and she appeared in explicit magazines and a range of television commercials, but her apparent relationship with Haumono suddenly faded when it became public news.

The whole thing, though, was really a ridiculous ploy by Haumono and his close friend Anthony Mundine, constructed to cause the termination of Haumono's contract with Canterbury-Bankstown so he could join Mundine at the St. George Dragons, where Mundine was the club's first-grade five-eighth. Reportedly, Haumono never even met with Richens while in England during his "pursuit of love" and simply waited it out, hoping his contract with Canterbury-Bankstown would be terminated. Mundine played the role of rescuer to his lovestruck pal by travelling to England and bringing Haumono back to Sydney, but the ruse was a massive failure because, despite their best efforts of secrecy, big mouths meant Canterbury-Bankstown quickly became aware it was all a sham. They refused to release Haumono from his contract and promptly dropped him from first grade, and any verbal agreement Haumono had with St. George was long gone.

It would take more than a decade for Mundine and Haumono to publicly come clean, and they were quick to blame immaturity, but sadly such blatant and extravagant dishonesty is not something even a young adult can just put down to naivety. They would both make public apologies, and as Richens's fame dwindled in Australia, she would return to England, but she could have spoken up at any time if she had wanted to.

It was all quite a spectacle in 1998, but it did create an opportunity for Balmain to sign Haumono for 1999, which they successfully did. It was easy enough for Balmain fans to forget Haumono's foolishness and concentrate on his devastating power, which in attack and defence would add further potency to Balmain's forward pack. It should be duly noted that up until 1998, Haumono had no notable prior history of poor behaviour. He was also known to be devoutly religious, a family-orientated person, and popular among his teammates.

Balmain also signed Haumono's former teammate, outside back Craig Hancock from Manly Warringah. Hancock had 172 first-grade appearances with them and had played a lot on the wing but could cover fullback or play in the centres. He had made his debut for Manly Warringah as a nineteen-year-old winger during Round 3 on Sunday, April 2, 1989, against the Knights in Newcastle, a game Newcastle won 14–0. Hancock played one game for the New South Wales Blues during the 1995 State of Origin series, but most importantly, he added a wealth of experience to a quite youthful Balmain backline. The 1999 season was Adam Nable's third at Balmain, and he knew both Hancock and Haumono well from his time at Manly Warringah. He felt both would add value to Balmain, saying, "The club culture, you want good people there and both of them [Hancock and Haumono] are good people" (Nable 2018).

Tyran Smith had become a bit of a journeyman by the time Balmain signed him for the 1999 season. He had appeared in seventy-three first-grade games for four different clubs since 1993 (South Sydney Rabbitohs, Hunter Mariners, North Queensland Cowboys, and the Auckland Warriors), but he had appeared in fifty-two games for South Sydney from 1993 to 1996. He made his first-grade debut for South Sydney during Round 17 on Sunday, July 25, 1993, at the Sydney Football Stadium, where the team took on Manly Warringah. Smith came off the bench during that game, and Manly Warringah won it 38–10. He played primarily as a winger in 1993, but as time went on, he established himself as a lock forward and occasionally played as a centre and often enough as a second rower. Smith's tall frame gave him a long stride, and he was difficult for opposing players to bring to the ground. He had also played for New Zealand and was yet another player that brought representative experience to Balmain.

Not all of Balmain's 1999 recruits arrived before the season began, and halfback Craig Field played his final first-grade game for Manly Warringah during Round 5 on April 3 and was in uniform for Balmain in Round 7 on April 18, which just happened to be against his former club. Field had made his first-grade debut for the South Sydney Rabbitohs during Round 21 on Sunday, August 19, 1990, coming off the bench against St. George Dragons at Kogarah Oval, and St. George won the game 46–24. By 1993, he was South Sydney's incumbent halfback, and he would make eighty-four appearances for South Sydney from 1990 to 1996 and fifty-four for Manly Warringah from 1997 to 1999. With 138 first-grade appearances, Field was a wealth of experience.

There were rumours amongst some Balmain fans that, as far back as 1996, the club was somewhat interested in recruiting Field but had not been able to compete with the offer made by Manly Warringah, which had secured Field's services in 1997. Danny Munk recalls, "There was talk Craig was looking for other opportunities…our board certainly wanted to make as much of the opportunity in '99 to get as high up on the rankings…where you [the club] finished in the '99 season was also part of that [competition's rationalisation] criteria…We were in many ways struggling for a halfback…there were conversations between the agent [Field's] and our club during the early part of '99, but he still had a contract with Manly…Manly weren't really that keen to let him go…we were very interested…fairly quickly we got to a point where between what

Manly were prepared to sign off on and pay because they still had a contract with Craig, and what we were prepared to pay for Craig [to complete the deal], and then he joined us before the halfway point of the season…He certainly had an impact straight away… Craig was quite a talent" (Munk 2018). Physically, Field was smaller in size, but he had so much heart and an admirable ability to get back up, no matter how heavy a tackle he had been on the receiving end of, and keep playing like it was nothing. "He just wanted to compete…he was like a kid in under-sevens…he competed all the time…it was awesome," said Balmain teammate Adam Nable (2018).

The signing of centre/winger John Carlaw was lauded somewhat in the media, as he was twenty-four years old and had made twenty-four appearances with the Melbourne Storm during their inaugural 1998 season. Melbourne's quick success had impressed many, and Carlaw had appeared in all but two of their regular-season games, as well as two of their three finals games. He made his first-grade debut during Round 4 on Saturday, March 22, 1997, for Super League club the Hunter Mariners, and their opponent was the North Queensland Cowboys. The Mariners won the game 38–10, and playing as a centre, Carlaw scored two tries on debut.

He had plenty of athleticism, and 1999 teammate Joel Caine remembers, "He was a great athlete, rock solid, terrific player…I remember we got asked to play on an A-grade cricket team…I said, 'how do you go [at cricket] J. C. [John Carlaw]?' and he said, 'Not that flash.' He asked me how do I go and I was pumping myself up. Anyway, [batting] I got a duck [scored zero runs] he got 145 or something…unbelievable athlete" (Caine 2018). Carlaw was also known to be a fairly capable basketball player, as well. Balmain wanted to add some proven spark to their outside backline, and

Carlaw was certainly a decent acquisition for the club.

Winger/fullback Joel Caine joined Balmain under some unique circumstances. "They signed three of us [from the St. George Dragons], a bloke named Brad Smith, Steve Price [and Caine]...the three of us signed together...Back in those days everything [training/playing] was going full-time and I was in an electrical apprenticeship...I'm on the phone to Wayne Pearce, and Wayne said, 'We need you to go full-time'...as we're having the conversation he's got me on speaker phone and the club electrician was fixing a light in his office as we were on the phone...[The club electrician said] 'I'll take him on' and I ended up working for the club [Balmain Leagues Club] as a staff member thanks to that conversation...I finished my trade there...I'm a very ordinary sparky [electrician] to the point where I'm so bad I can't fall back on it," said Caine with a laugh (2018).

Caine had made his first-grade debut with the St. George Dragons during Round 23 on Friday, August 14, 1998, at Bruce Stadium against the Canberra Raiders. He came off the bench for St. George, but Canberra snuck away with a 28–24 win. Caine, though, would make club history as the final player to debut in first grade for the St. George Dragons. For Caine, looking back on the game, it had "massive significance...one of the first games I saw...Canterbury played Canberra...I was ten or eleven...Canberra were my favourite team as a kid...Ricky Stuart was my favourite player...my debut...my very first touch was [catching] a towering Ricky Stuart torpedo kick...I just about dropped it [the football], I've got no idea to this day how I caught it...Brett Mullins, I'm still convinced to this day he actually did a one-on-one steal on me [of the ball off Caine], somehow I ended up with the ball back...it's almost as if he [Mullins] felt sorry for me" (Caine 2018). Caine appeared in three first-grade games for St. George in 1998, which included their finals (qualifying finals) game, which the Canterbury-Bankstown Bulldogs won 20–12. Caine would be competing with other outside backs to play either on a wing or at fullback for Balmain, and at twenty years old, he was one of the younger players.

Brad Smith usually played second row, but he was a versatile player that could cover lock or the front row if need be. From 1995 to 1998, he had played twenty-seven first-grade games for St. George and usually came off the bench. He had made his debut during Round 16 on Sunday, July 16, 1995, at the Sydney Cricket Ground against the Western Suburbs Magpies. He came off the bench, and St. George won the game 25–12. Smith would add depth to Balmain's forward pack.

Five-eighth Steven Price completed the trio of St. George players with prior first-grade experience. He made his first-grade debut during Round 14 on Sunday, June 22, 1997, at Kogarah Oval against the Illawarra Steelers. He came off the bench, and Illawarra won the game 12–10. He appeared in nine first-grade games in 1997 but didn't play at that level in 1998 due to injury. Price was noted to have a good passing and kicking game, and the five-eighth depth at Balmain would be helpful.

Michael Ostini was another utility forward that could play in the front or second row. He joined Balmain having appeared in thirty-one first-grade games from 1996 to 1998. He had made his first-grade debut as a Sydney City Rooster during Round 15 on Sunday, July 14, 1996, at North Sydney Oval. Sydney City managed to nudge out the North Sydney Bears 30–25 that game, and Ostini came off the bench. He'd play the next week for Sydney City in his only other first-grade game with them before joining the South Sydney Rabbitohs for 1997. He stayed on there in 1998, and twenty-nine of his first-grade games were with South Sydney. He added some size and mobility to the forward pack.

Garth Wood came from a rugby league family, as his dad, Barry, had played for Newtown, South Sydney, and North Sydney from 1970 to 1979. Garth's brother Nathan had played for Balmain from 1993 to 1994 and had joined the Sydney City Roosters in 1995, which was still his club as of 1999. Garth was a utility back that could cover wing, centre, or fullback. He had made his first-grade debut during Round 16 on Sunday, July 20, 1997, against the St. George Dragons at Kogarah Oval. It was an agonisingly close game, with St. George winning 29–28. From 1997 to 1998, he had appeared in six first-grade games for South Sydney. When he joined Balmain, Wood was twenty years old, and his youth and ability to play different positions at the very least offered Balmain some spark off the bench.

Justin Yeo could play as a centre or in the second row, and in 1998 he had made his first-grade debut with the North Sydney Bears during Round 12 on Saturday, May 30, 1998, where he came off the bench at Shark Park, and Cronulla-Sutherland won the game 16–12. He came to Balmain with that first-grade experience under his belt and wanting to contribute to his new club.

Nick Shaw was the last of the players with previous first-grade experience to join Balmain in 1999, but he did so having made his first-grade debut as a North Sydney Bear during Round 7 on Friday, April 16, 1999, at the Sydney Football Stadium against the Sydney City Roosters. He came off the bench in a game Sydney City won 28–16. He joined Balmain during the 1999 season, and as a five-eighth, he filled a position Balmain wanted to have choice in.

Balmain had recruited plenty of players with first-grade experience and of varying ages to the club for 1999, and those players would complement the incumbent first-grade squad, as well as those that were aiming to get a chance in first grade from the club's lower grades. They had quite a task ahead of them, as Balmain aimed to be competitive in the newly reduced seventeen-team competition, plus they had the added pressure of knowing it would be a fourteen-team competition for the year 2000, and the club's performance in 1999 would be a factor in whether they would be part of that fourteen-team competition.

# CHAPTER 5

# SHARK ATTACK AND TURNAROUND

The 1998 retirement of front rower Paul Sironen meant that the captaincy of Balmain was open for 1999, and hooker/lock Darren Senter was appointed the duty. Having played thirty games for the Canterbury-Bankstown Bulldogs between 1992 and 1994, Senter then joined the Sydney Tigers and made his debut off the bench during Round 1 on Sunday, March 12, 1995, at Parramatta Stadium. Playing at what was their home venue, Sydney Tigers faced Sydney City Roosters, and they won the game 24–18. Inclusive of the 1998 season, Senter had played seventy-six first-grade games for Sydney/Balmain Tigers, and he was noted for his fearless competitiveness on the field.

A new captain and season provided a fresh start for Balmain. The knowledge that the competition would be reduced from seventeen clubs to fourteen for the 2000 season was well noted, yet according to Balmain's CEO Danny Munk, "The mood was positive…it wasn't that anyone was giving up…we always knew one way or another the Tigers would always exist…we were going into

1999 to put our best foot forward…the best way to generate sponsorship and dollars is to have a competitive team…Wayne Pearce and the board were certainly very focused on that" (Munk 2018).

The season began for Balmain on Sunday, March 7, at Shark Park, where they would take on the Cronulla-Sutherland Sharks. The clubs met only once during the 1998 season, and Balmain had won the game 11–10. In the final moments of that game, Cronulla-Sutherland centre Russell Richardson made a break and flirted with the sideline before scoring what appeared to be a game-winning try, but it was ruled by a touch judge that Richardson's foot had made contact with the sideline, and the try was disallowed. Richardson was adamant his foot had stayed within the sideline, but the decision was final, and the win was Balmain's. Video replay, though, didn't help the decision and if anything supported that the try should have been awarded. It would prove to be a very tough loss for Cronulla-Sutherland, because they finished the 1998 season in eleventh position, with twelve wins, one draw, and eleven losses, which was just one win short of qualifying for the season's top-ten finals. Had they beat Balmain, they would have finished eighth, because their drawn game and points differential would have put them above the clubs positioned ninth and tenth. Cronulla-Sutherland had no doubt not forgotten how costly their 1998 loss to Balmain had been.

The advertising campaign for the 1999 NRL season consisted of a poem by Thomas Keneally called, "Ode to Rugby League," which Keneally (a staunch Manly Warringah Sea Eagles supporter) read over some images of simulated rugby league play. As a television advertisement for rugby league, it was certainly different from the fast/high impact game-day action footage, complemented with part or all of a popular chart song as background sound, that was used in the past. From Keneally's poem, a notable line that appeared twice was "Blow that whistle, ref." When Cronulla-Sutherland and Balmain met for their Round 1 game, the referee that day was Moghseen Jadwat, and he had quite a busy time blowing his whistle, awarding tries to Cronulla-Sutherland. At halftime, Cronulla-Sutherland had a 20–0 lead, and at fulltime they had won convincingly with 44–0.

It was a heavy loss to start a season, and it was Balmain/Sydney Tigers' worst Round 1 game loss of the entire decade. They had had their share of Round 1 losses during the 1990s, but 1999 was a thumping and appeared out of character for Balmain. Adam Nable came off the bench for Balmain that day, and he felt there were circumstances that needed to be considered: "The week before the start of the season in Hawks Nest we're running sand hills…we're getting flogged…Junior [Wayne Pearce] got in this ex-SAS guy (Royal Australian Special Air Service Regiment) that had done three tours of Vietnam and one in Borneo, and he's talking about mental toughness and all this sort of stuff…we'd been doing these sand hills… probably not the best preparation to go into the start of a season… [by the first game] everyone should have been jumping out of their skin, but we were a bit flat…it was like we did something you do at the start of preseason to flog you…I remember spewing during the training…you shouldn't be spewing up the week before [the start of the season]" (Nable 2018). The result was disappointing, but the game would represent the Balmain Tigers' debut of fullback/winger Joel Caine, centre John Carlaw, winger Craig Hancock, front rower Jason Lowrie, second rower Solomon Haumono (who suffered an elbow injury during the game), and utility Justin Yeo, who came off the bench.

Balmain needed to rebound quickly, because for Round 2 they

would face the Melbourne Storm at Leichhardt Oval, and Melbourne was a red-hot team. The 1999 expectations for Melbourne were that they could finish even better than their third-place 1998 debut season. Balmain only met Melbourne once during the 1998 season, which was at Leichhardt Oval, and Melbourne won that game 25–16. Melbourne's Round 1 game for the 1999 season was against the Penrith Panthers at Melbourne's home, Olympic Park, on Friday, March 5. It was a tight game, with Melbourne leading 8–4 at halftime, but they ran away with the game during the second half, piling on 24 points to win 32–10. It was Saturday night, March 13, when Balmain took on Melbourne at Leichhardt Oval, and Melbourne were easy favourites to win the game. Making their Balmain Tigers debut that night were second rower Brad Smith and forward Tyran Smith, who came off the bench. (Despite sharing the same surname, they were not relatives.)

It is often said that reaching the highest level of any sport is an incredible achievement, but making it back to those heights can be considered even more phenomenal. Winger Chris Morcombe appeared in five first-grade games for Balmain in 1994, and his final for that season was during Round 22 on Sunday, August 28, at (Brisbane's) ANZ Stadium, where they played the Brisbane Broncos, and it was the final game of Balmain's 1994 season. Balmain were guaranteed last place on the competition ladder of sixteen teams—and the dreaded wooden spoon—regardless of whether they could miraculously beat Brisbane.

Balmain won just four games in 1994, and Morcombe was still a teenager that year at nineteen years old. In attendance for Balmain's final game of the 1994 season was an impressive crowd of 47,486 people, and Balmain would become Sydney Tigers in 1995, playing their home games at Parramatta Stadium. With the changes approaching, it was reasonable to conclude that it was Balmain's final-ever first-grade game in the then New South Wales Rugby League, and Morcombe was a starter for that game as a winger. It was a tough game for Balmain, as Brisbane won emphatically 41–6. Thereafter, Balmain was thought to be extinct, but they of course returned to being Balmain in 1997.

Morcombe hadn't appeared in first grade since that Brisbane game on August 28, 1994, and he was twenty-three years old when Balmain faced Melbourne on March 13, 1999. In total, 1,658 days, or four years, six months, and thirteen days, had passed between his appearances in first grade. Regardless of the team result, at a personal level it was a momentous occasion for Morcombe.

Prior to the Melbourne Storm game in 1999, Ben Duckworth had played lock in all but one of his nineteen first-grade appearances with Balmain since 1998, up to and including Round 1 in 1999. The only exception was him coming off the bench for Balmain during Round 13 in 1998, and he covered a few positions but notably second row and lock. Back in Round 1 of the 1995 season, when Duckworth was playing for the Illawarra Steelers, he started that game at five-eighth, but that was his only prior listed start in that position during his first-grade career up to 1999. Since joining Balmain in 1998, Duckworth had thrived: "[He] was a great player…he was one of my mates on that team and I spent a lot of time with him," said Adam Nable (2018). Balmain CEO Danny Munk recalled (2018), "I remember him as a highly intelligent, talented individual." And even though he was new to the club, winger/fullback Joel Caine quickly noticed Duckworth, as well: "Very, very skilful…he had the best kicking game in the competition…he grew up playing a lot of AFL [Australian Rules Football]…he was supremely talented…he was easy to be around" (Caine 2018).

For Balmain's Round 2 game in 1999 against Melbourne, Duckworth was selected to start the game at five-eighth for the second time in his career to date. Seventeen players all helped contribute to help Balmain beat Melbourne 16–6 that Saturday night, but Duckworth had done a fine job marshalling Balmain's attack with his clever kicking and passing game, and he was also a danger to the opposition with the ball in his hands running, which helped him score his first and only try for the 1999 season that night. New recruits Brad Smith and John Carlaw scored a try each, and it was extra special for Carlaw to score one against his former club Melbourne. For Smith, he had scored during his Balmain first-grade debut game, and it was the third and final try of his first-grade career. The win was an instant revival for Balmain's 1999 season, and Adam Nable, who had started the game at lock, proudly recollected, "That was a great win...on your day you know you can compete with anyone" (Nable 2018).

Balmain's Round 3 opponent was the North Queensland Cowboys, and it was another Saturday night game at Leichhardt Oval on March 20. New recruit and utility Garth Wood made his Balmain Tigers first-grade debut off the bench that evening in a game Balmain won 26–18. Chris Morcombe hadn't scored a try during his five appearances with Balmain in 1994, but he had a busy night against North Queensland, running in two tries to get his first-grade career tally moving. It seemed the new recruits wanted to wow the Balmain faithful, which were just 5,969 in attendance that night, as John Carlaw made it two tries in two consecutive games, and Joel Caine helped with fourteen points, which consisted of his maiden first-grade try, and five goal-kick conversions.

Balmain had now played three games and won two, and the effort on the field by the players was always complemented by good instruction and mentoring. "Junior [Wayne Pearce] is great…one of his real assets was getting people up and getting them motivated for the game…everything was based on defence and we tried really hard to work on that…I think we had confidence, and we could beat anyone," said Nable (2018) when considering the team's performance in Rounds 1–3. Two wins from three games surprisingly put Balmain in only the tenth spot on the NRL's seventeen-club competition ladder. The top eight teams by the end of the regular season would qualify for the finals, and making the finals was potentially a matter of survival beyond the 1999 season. Winning, though, had helped minimise media talk of amalgamating Balmain with another club, and at that early stage of the 1999 season, it seemed to be of little benefit worrying too much about the fourteen-club competition for the 2000 NRL season, because so much of 1999 was still ahead of Balmain.

Balmain were keen to make it three consecutive wins. Their Round 4 opponent was the Parramatta Eels, and the Eels were expected to finish among the leaders in 1999. Those expectations were well justified, because Parramatta finished the regular season in second place, and they came close to a grand final appearance when they lost their preliminary finals game to the Melbourne Storm, with the Storm winning 26–18. Going into Round 4, Balmain and Parramatta both had won two games from three, which added to their already spirited rivalry. The game was played at Parramatta Stadium on Saturday, March 27, and a crowd of 17,253 was in attendance that night.

For Balmain front rower Adam Starr, it would be the final time in his first-grade career that he would make a run-on start. Going into the 1999 season, Starr had made thirty-three first-grade appearances with Sydney/Balmain Tigers, and even though front rowers often have height and size, Starr was taller than most and was broad from head to foot. He would appear in six more games during the 1999 season for Balmain coming off the bench, but his final first-grade start was for an intense game against Parramatta. Parramatta went into halftime with a 12–8 lead, and Balmain was pushing a team with more fancied players on their home ground.

Adam Starr and the rest of Balmain's forward pack were going toe-to-toe with Parramatta's hard, skilful forwards, consisting of Jim Dymock and Jarrod McCracken and rising young talents Michael Vella and Nathan Hindmarsh. Front rower Mark Tookey played some of his best rugby league for Parramatta, and he took some effort to stop with the ball in his hands. Parramatta's hooker, Dean Schifilliti, went into the 1999 season with 154 first-grade appearances under his belt. Even though all the point-scoring during the game was done by Parramatta's and Balmain's backlines, the forwards ground it out. Starr and all of Balmain's players used their might and experience to try and keep pace with Parramatta, but during the second half of the game, Parramatta ran away with it, and the final score was 26–12.

Balmain could take away from the game that they had been competitive for at least half of it, and while a win would have pushed them further up the ladder, the fact they had two wins from four games was decent, and their next game was back at Leichhardt Oval, where they would take on the Auckland Warriors. Even though Auckland was a bit of an enigma when it came to consistency, they had a good supply of hefty, gritty players that took pride in adding some extra physicality to the game.

# CHAPTER 6

# MOSTLY WINNING

Balmain's Round 5 encounter with the Auckland Warriors would be the first and only time the two clubs would play an NRL first-grade game at Leichhardt Oval. It was Saturday night on April 3, and Adam Nable started the game at lock. "Every time you played Auckland you had to brace yourself because they were big and they were physical," recalled Nable (2018). Playing in the second row that night for Auckland was Tony Tuimavave, and Balmain's halfback, Michael Gillett, found himself on the end of a jolting Tuimavave tackle. Gillett had also received plenty of attention from other players on the Auckland team, which would contribute to an early night for him, and he would miss Balmain's Round 6 game, as well.

Gillett was nudging close to one hundred first-grade appearances, and having him off the field meant five-eighth Ben Duckworth had additional responsibilities in terms of managing Balmain's attacking plays. Balmain rose to the challenge, though, with forward Solomon Haumono coming off the bench to score a try, and Nable scored one, too. Joel Caine converted four goals from five attempts, and Duckworth's field goal ensured Balmain won the game 17–8. Containing Auckland to just eight points confirmed Balmain had plenty of muscle, to keep such an explosive team to less than ten points. Three wins from five games put Balmain on the plus side of the win-loss ledger, but only as far as eleventh of the seventeen teams on the competition ladder. To crack the top eight, they needed to keep winning, but other clubs were desperate to get there, too.

In 1998 Balmain played the North Sydney Bears once that season, during Round 22 on August 8 at North Sydney Oval, and North Sydney won the game 22–6. To add a bit of extra sting to the loss, former Balmain boy Glenn Morrison came off the bench for North Sydney and scored a try against his former club. Balmain's last win over North Sydney was during Round 7 of the 1997 season, which was a gutsy 9–7 victory on Friday night, April 18, at Leichhardt Oval. There was a reasonable perception that Balmain had a habit of finding something extra when it came to home games at sacred Leichhardt Oval, but going into their Round 6 game at Leichhardt Oval on Saturday night, April 10, 1999, their opponent North Sydney had won three of the four games they had played. North Sydney had also had a bye for Round 3, which meant they had played one less game than Balmain, and some might say that they went into the game fresher and slightly more confident than Balmain.

North Sydney's halfback and five-eighth combination consisted of Jason Taylor (halfback) and Michael Buettner (five-eighth), both of whom had representative experience, having played for the New South Wales Blues at different times, and Buettner had played for Australia. Taylor had over two hundred first-grade appearances, and Buettner had over 150. Balmain had Adam Nable starting at halfback to cover for Michael Gillett, and Ben Duckworth was at five-eighth. Nable and Duckworth were matched up against a very experienced pair in Taylor and Buettner, and at every possible chance, North Sydney got in the face of Duckworth to smother his kicking game and to also restrict his movement, thus reducing his attacking potency with the ball in his hands. Taylor was also able to charge down and regather the ball from an attempted clearing kick by Duckworth, and Taylor scoring a try added to a frustrating night for Duckworth.

North Sydney's fullback Matt Seers's blistering speed and solid tackling that night further smothered Balmain's attack, as the slightest of attacking line-break made by a Balmain player was nearly instantly extinguished by the ability of Seers to be on top of them before they could gain much speed or metres. Balmain couldn't keep up with North Sydney's clinical play, and the 26–4 score in North Sydney's favour confirmed the dominance of their performance. The loss shifted Balmain from eleventh to twelfth on the competition ladder, but three wins and three losses was still something to work with.

Despite the result, the Round 6 encounter against North Sydney had some personal significance for young Balmain second rower Troy Wozniak, as he made his first-grade debut off the bench, and making his debut at Leichhardt Oval was something extra for a tough forward who had been a standout player in Balmain's lower grades. Wozniak was a starting second rower in Balmain's under-20s 1997 grand final team, which faced a hot young crop of Sydney City Roosters players, such as Justin Brooker, Anthony Minichiello, Chad Halliday, Ben MacDougall, Damien Mostyn, Justin Smith, Hayes Lauder, Andrew Lomu, Peter Cusack, and Trent Robinson. All of them would play first grade, and Minichiello would go on to have a phenomenal career, which included 302 first-grade appearances. Minichiello, though, had a bit of an ordinary game in the 1997 under-20s grand final, dropping the ball a few times, and this gave Balmain some crucial field position. Balmain won 13–12, and Wozniak contributed with spirited effort and notably solid defence to help contain a more fancied opponent. On April 10, 1999, he broke through to first grade, and he would appear in one more game for Balmain, which coincidentally was Balmain's corresponding game against North Sydney during Round 13 at North Sydney Oval. Wozniak was subsequently Balmain's initial first-grade debutant for the 1999 season by debuting during Round 6. His progression through Balmain's lower grades and all his hard work over the years earned him the promotion to first grade. Wozniak's first-grade career would span from 1999 to 2003, and he would appear in thirty-eight games.

So Wozniak making his first-grade debut was one positive to come from Round 6, but things weren't getting any easier for Balmain, as their Round 7 opponent was Manly Warringah Sea Eagles at Leichhardt Oval. Manly Warringah had played in three consecutive grand finals from 1995 to 1997, but by 1998 they had faded, just scraping into the top ten–placed team finals in tenth place of the twenty-team competition, and they were the first team eliminated from the 1998 finals, as the Canberra Raiders won their qualifying finals game 17–4. The 1999 season had got off to a horrible start for Manly Warringah, as they had lost all six games they played, and a club desperate for a win can be a highly unpredictable opponent. On paper, Manly Warringah still had some high-calibre players, with numerous state and international representative honours amongst them. They had Terry Hill, Geoff Toovey, Steve Menzies, Nik Kosef, Cliff Lyons, and John Hopoate as the most decorated in terms of representative experience. It was therefore difficult to understand why they were winless, and from Manly Warringah's point of view, playing against Balmain, who were coming off a convincing loss at home to North Sydney, was a chance to notch up that maiden win for the 1999 season.

It was completely uncharacteristic for Manly Warringah to be doing so poorly, because from the 1970s right through to nearly all of the 1990s, they had been a highly competitive club, winning the 1972, 1973, 1976, 1978, 1987, and 1996 grand finals. Pressure to perform was everywhere, and in amongst the calamity, their halfback Craig Field had been dropped as starting halfback for their Round 5 game against South Sydney Rabbitohs, as he was named on the bench. Rumours were loud that Field wanted a new opportunity, and when he wasn't named for their first-grade game for Round 6 against the Canberra Raiders, the talk was that Field would be joining Balmain. When he was named at halfback for Balmain for their Round 7 game against Manly Warringah, it became a fact.

Since the departure of Gary Freeman from Balmain following the 1991 season, some might say Balmain hadn't been able to fully replace his class and skill at halfback. Field joined Balmain with 138 first-grade appearances and a well-deserved reputation as a determined player with a good supply of clever play. It doesn't happen often in sport, but Field was one of those few that would play their first game for their new club against their former team. Perhaps even more unique was the fact that it had happened during the course of the season, as rugby league for the most part had a history of players usually joining another club after the season's end.

It seemed like a strategic disadvantage to allow a player that only two weeks earlier was playing for Manly Warringah to be able to play against his old club (as would be permitted as part of the negotiations between the two clubs). As a halfback Field was a key playmaker, and he knew so much about Manly Warringah's style of play, so some prudent governance by Manly Warringah might have prompted them to place a caveat of a one-week hold on the release of Field from his contract at Manly Warringah, thus ensuring he didn't play his former club immediately upon his release. However, it was possible Manly Warringah had so many other pressures that immediately releasing Field was a smoother, easier pathway for them. There were also those mutterings from some fans of the game that Manly Warringah had put such little value on Field's playing form from the 1999 season that they simply didn't care if he played his first game for Balmain against Manly Warringah.

Field's transition to Balmain was instant, and so was the value of his skills, as his passing and kicking game was superb, and Balmain looked revitalised with him leading their attack. It was a sunny Sunday afternoon on April 18 at Leichhardt Oval, and it was like the week before against North Sydney had been over a year ago, as Balmain took it to Manly Warringah and won the game 18–12. Adam Nable played hooker for Balmain that afternoon and said of the victory, "It was awesome! A great feeling…and an awesome atmosphere" (Nable 2018).

With seven consecutive losses, Manly Warringah's coach, Bob Fulton, was thereafter replaced by Peter Sharp. Based on his incredible playing career, Fulton was inducted as an Immortal of the game in 1981, which made him one of the first four inductees (the others were Clive Churchill, Reg Gasnier, and Johnny Raper). He had coached Manly Warringah to grand final wins in 1987 and 1996 and was regarded for many years as one of the game's best coaches, yet perhaps there was something ironic about the fact that the last first-grade game he coached for Manly Warringah involved a player that only two weeks earlier appeared in first grade for him and was a key architect of Balmain's Round 7 victory. Craig Field's debut game for Balmain was a stunning success for him and a brilliant win for the club.

The game presented its share of other personal milestones, too, as it would be Balmain centre/five-eighth Jacin Sinclair's first appearance of the 1999 season in first grade, coming off the bench. Sinclair made his first-grade debut for Balmain during Round 11 on Sunday, June 9, 1991, at Leichhardt Oval, and he partnered Tim Brasher in the centres that afternoon. Balmain took on the Gold Coast Seagulls that day, and Sinclair's first-grade career began with a win, as Balmain won the game 14–6. Sinclair was nineteen years old when he made his first-grade debut. He and Adam Nable would become teammates at Balmain in 1998, and Nable observed, "Sinclair had enormous talent...he grew up playing against my brother Matthew...he [Sinclair] was at Holy Cross [College] Ryde...he was a super talented football player...He'd go out and do things most guys could only dream of...he was a really good bloke as well...if he was available you wanted him playing five-eighth or centre because he just had that presence on the field where you felt like he could do something...no ego, never thought he was better than other people...You've got to have a good dynamic in a team environment, you've all got to get along...be on that same page...he ticked all the boxes, he was great value...told great stories, being in the locker room was awesome" (Nable 2018).

Back in 1993, Sinclair was selected for the New South Wales City representative team, and he was in the prime of his career at twenty-one years old. He had also looked all set to play for NSW Blues in State of Origin, and only an injury stopped him. He joined South Sydney Rabbitohs in 1994 and played there through 1996, then in 1997 he joined Sydney City Roosters. In 1998 he returned to Balmain, and club CEO Danny Munk recalls, "I got to know Jacin when he had come back into the club…it was very obvious not only was he talented, but he was just passionate about rugby league…he was also passionate about his family…in that period he was at the club I saw nothing but positives…as a human being he was a good person" (Munk 2018).

Sinclair appeared in three games for Balmain in 1998, and by 1999 he was one of the more experienced guys at the club at twenty-seven years old. As a new player to the club for the 1999 season, Joel Caine got to know veterans like Sinclair, and "he [Sinclair] was the most laidback character I think I've ever played with…a good heartbeat around the team as well…he was always having a laugh… We'd have a dress-up night, you had to go as a 'B' or a 'T'…my girlfriend at the time and I, we went as [Don] Bradman and [Mark] Taylor a couple of cricketers…he [Sinclair] turned up as *Baywatch* [an American action drama television series about lifeguards], all he had on was a pair of red togs [swimming bathers] that was sort of him, larger than life," said Caine (2018).

The 18–12 Balmain win against Manly Warringah during Round 7 in 1999 was Sinclair's first win on a Balmain first-grade team since rejoining the club in 1998, and considering that the last time he played on a winning Balmain team was Round 19 at Leichhardt Oval on Sunday, August 8, 1993, when Balmain won over Penrith Panthers 28–12, it had been 2,079 days, or five years, eight months, and ten days, for him between enjoying first-grade victories as a Balmain Tiger. Winning was always a team effort, yet a win has its own significance to each player on the field.

Sinclair was an experienced campaigner, and around him there was some youth, as one of the youngsters coming off the bench that day with him was front rower Richard Villasanti. At the time, Villasanti was still eighteen years old, and he would turn nineteen on May 20. Villasanti was the second player to make his first-grade debut for Balmain during the 1999 season. He nearly scored on debut, but he just lost control of the ball over the try line; however, having a win on debut was a great way to commence his first-grade career. Villasanti would become known for his impact as a rugged front rower, and he would go on to appear in 116 first-grade games.

For Round 8, Balmain had their final of four consecutive games at Leichhardt. Their opponent that day was Western Suburbs Magpies, and it was another Sunday afternoon in the sun on April 25, 1999. It was a good day for Balmain's veteran winger, Craig Hancock, as he scored a hat trick of tries, and it was the first and only time during his first-grade career that he would score three tries in one game. At the time, Hancock was twenty-nine years old, and he would turn thirty on June 10, yet despite being an older player on Balmain's backline, he added value as an experienced outside back. Balmain scored twenty-eight points that afternoon, and combined it came from both centres, the wingers, and the fullback. Centres John Carlaw and Jason Webber had a try each, and winger Chris Morcombe had one, as well, while fullback Joel Caine added four points with two successful goal kicks. It was Balmain's day, as they won 28–16, and the win shot them up to sixth on the competition ladder, placing them in the sixth spot of the competition's top eight of seventeen teams. If they could keep a place in the top eight, they'd surprise a lot of experts, and it would no doubt be helpful for their future beyond the 1999 season.

Adam Nable was Balmain's hooker for the game against Western Suburbs, and it had its share of grit and implication. "I think I tried to hit [with a tackle] Harvey Howard and I thought I broke my shoulder…Playing at Leichhardt with two foundation clubs with all the talk that was going on [about merging]…it was good to win, it's always good to get a win," said Nable (2018). Englishman Harvey Howard was a bullocking front rower who could rampage through a defensive line, and plenty of players had come off second-best trying to stop him. Western Suburbs had plenty of good players in their forward pack, which included but was not limited to hooker Ciriaco Mescia, front rower John Skandalis, and lock Steve Georgallis. Centre Kevin McGuinness and fullback Brett Hodgson were key spark plug players when it came to attack for Western Suburbs.

Even though Western Suburbs had only won one game from five played going into their game against Balmain, they had pressure on them to win, as the axe was swinging to reduce the number of clubs to fourteen for the 2000 season, and Western Suburbs had finished the 1998 season in last place of the twenty-team competition, with only four wins. Balmain was vulnerable, too, but continuing to win and hopefully staying within the top eight was one way to distance themselves from conversations about clubs that might face the chop or would be a candidate for a merge after the 1999 season. All the players could do to pitch Balmain's future beyond 1999 was to go out there and play their guts out to try to win each game.

Five-eighth Steven Price made his first-grade Balmain club debut off the bench against Western Suburbs, and it had been a long road back to first grade for him. At nineteen years old, he had made his first-grade debut with the St. George Dragons during Round 14 on Sunday, June 22, 1997, when he came off the bench for St. George. Their opponent that day was Illawarra Steelers, and Illawarra managed to grind out a 12–10 win. Price would appear in eight more first-grade games for St. George in 1997, but he didn't appear in first grade at all during the 1998 season due to injury. His final first-grade appearance for St. George was on August 29, 1997, and returning to first grade with Balmain on April 25, 1999, constituted 604 days, or one year, seven months, and twenty-seven days, between first-grade appearances. He was twenty-one years old by then, which in rugby league terms was still quite young, but such an absence from appearing in first grade can test the resolve of any player to continue on with their career. To Price's credit, he kept going, and his new opportunity at Balmain quickly proved rewarding. The win against Western Suburbs was for the team, but for Price it was a personal victory, too, as reaching first grade is one huge challenge, but getting back to that level after a long recovery from injury is its own special achievement.

Having beaten Manly Warringah the week before, Balmain in their win over Western Suburbs made it their second back-to-back win streak of the season, but it would be the last time they would win consecutive games. The next five games for Balmain would go some way towards changing the mood of their season.

# CHAPTER 7

# FIVE TOUGH GAMES

For Round 9 on Saturday night, May 1, 1999, Balmain made the trip up to Townsville to play the North Queensland Cowboys at their home, Dairy Farmers Stadium. The local heat and humidity is often regarded as a home-ground advantage. Those arriving in Townsville by plane quickly find themselves greeted by greater heat or humidity or both compared to the cooler southern cities, such as Sydney and Melbourne.

Sydney/Balmain Tigers had only beaten North Queensland in Townsville once since 1995, when North Queensland joined the competition. It was during Round 13 on Saturday, June 24, 1995, at North Queensland's then-named Stockland Stadium that the Sydney Tigers won 28–14. They also beat North Queensland 38–16 during Round 3 of the 1995 season at Parramatta Stadium. Sydney Tigers didn't catch much of a break, having to play them in Townsville during Round 3 in 1996, because the local summer humidity was still lingering about, and the Tigers weren't even able to score a try, with North Queensland winning 17–2. They bounced back for their home 1996 encounter at Parramatta Stadium and edged North Queensland out by winning 18–16. In 1997 North Queensland didn't face Balmain, because they played in the Super League, and in 1998 North Queensland won 26–2 in Townsville during Round 2, and Balmain rebounded at Leichhardt Oval during Round 18, winning 18–0. Given that Balmain had won their first encounter for 1999 with North Queensland 26–18 during Round 3 at Leichhardt Oval, they had a task ahead of them to replicate the 1995 Sydney Tigers, in terms of winning both their home and away games against North Queensland.

After their Round 9 game against North Queensland, Balmain still had three more games to play to reach the halfway point of the 1999 season, but they hadn't yet recorded a win away from home. North Queensland was having a bit of a struggling season, and at the conclusion of Round 8, they sat at fifteenth on the seventeen-club competition ladder, with one win and a draw. It just so happened that North Queensland's win was during Round 7, and their draw occurred in Round 8. Even though North Queensland had lost five consecutive games up to and including Round 6, Balmain would be taking on a more confident North Queensland team. Balmain's choices to guide their attack at halfback and five-eighth were a bit slim due to injury/unavailability of Craig Field, Michael Gillett, and Ben Duckworth. It did, however, create an opportunity for James Webster to make his first-grade debut at halfback, and Steven Price would make his first run-on start as a Balmain Tiger at five-eighth.

While one play can rarely be attributed as the sole cause of a result, it was difficult to ignore the significance of North Queensland winger Brian Jellick's "never give up" try. Balmain's fullback, Joel Caine, shadowed the ball inside Balmain's in-goal area, and the ball had rolled deep into the in-goal area, courtesy of a North Queensland attacking kick. Caine watched the ball, hoping it would roll over the dead-ball line and possession of it would then be Balmain's with a twenty-metre line restart. If North Queensland players in pursuit of the ball got too close, Caine could kick the ball over the dead-ball line. Balmain would have to dropkick the ball from their goal line, which would put North Queensland back on the attack but nevertheless give Balmain a chance to further defend with the aim of thwarting North Queensland from scoring a try. Caine kept shadowing the ball, and all he needed was a few more seconds for the ball to roll over the dead-ball line, but Brian Jellick was sprinting after the ball, and he dived for it with an outstretched hand, miraculously grounding the ball for a North Queensland try. Caine couldn't believe it, but the video-replay was conclusive.

North Queensland won the game 20–14, and the difference was one converted try, yet the final score didn't reflect North Queensland's dominance. They scored four tries to Balmain's two, but North Queensland only converted two from six goal kicks, and Balmain converted three from four, thanks to the goal-kicking of Joel Caine. Interestingly, Steven Price and Richard Villasanti scored each of Balmain's tries, and whilst the team's winning the game was the most important outcome, it was still a personal milestone for Villasanti to score his maiden NRL first-grade try coming off the bench for Balmain. For Price, it would be his first NRL try scored as a Balmain Tiger and the final time he would score a try at NRL first-grade level.

It was a tough loss for Balmain, but they were missing some experienced players, and others weren't at full strength. Solomon Haumono started in the second row for Balmain against North Queensland, and it would be his final first-grade appearance as a Balmain Tiger. He had injured his elbow during Round 1, and his season was limited to eight games. His robustness and know-how as a player would be instantly missed.

Balmain had the bye for Round 10, and it was handy to have a week off for injured players to hopefully recover. It was also a chance for Balmain to prepare for their game against 1998 minor premiers and grand final winners the Brisbane Broncos. In 1998 Balmain had a 10–10 draw with Brisbane when they met during Round 20 at Leichhardt Oval, and on Sunday, May 16, 1999, they would meet again for their Round 11 fixture at Leichhardt Oval. The time off from the bye had ensured that Craig Field was available for selection, and he started the game at halfback for Balmain, with Steven Price at five-eighth. Brisbane was stacked with Queensland State of Origin players, and plenty had also played for Australia, too. Some of the big names included Tonie Carroll, Wendell Sailor, Kevin Walters, Shane Webcke, and Brad Thorn.

The list of players making their first-grade debut as Balmain Tigers continued to grow, with Hayes Lauder coming off the bench for Balmain. Lauder could play front or second row, and he was making his debut against a big and mobile Brisbane forward pack. Probably not quite a baptism of fire for Lauder, but certainly a tough and well-regarded group of Brisbane forwards would be on the other side of the field, and in sport there seems to be an uncanny tendency for rookies to receive extra attention. Notwithstanding this, Lauder found himself participating in a tight game, and it was quite reminiscent of the 1998 draw, only this time Balmain was clinging to a 10–6 lead and the game was nearly over.

It was a beautiful possibility that Balmain could beat Brisbane and Lauder start his first-grade career with a win that few experts would have predicted. All the Balmain players and the crowd of 13,236 could taste that win, and the Monday newspapers would make Balmain the sporting headline with a nice big colour action photograph and "High of the Tiger" or "Balmain Tame Broncos" in big capital letters—but alas, Brisbane centre Tonie Carroll knew how to break hearts.

At halftime of the 1998 grand final, Canterbury-Bankstown Bulldogs led 12–10, and playing lock for Brisbane was Tonie Carroll. His speed and strength caused havoc in the second half, and there was a chorus of people that considered him a key spark plug that contributed to twenty-eight unanswered points scored by Brisbane during the second half of the game, and he scored one of their tries. Brisbane won 38–12, with one of the most convincing second-half performances in grand final history.

Balmain hadn't lined-up against Carroll when the clubs met in 1998, and it was probably just as well. In 1999, even though the game was nearly over and Balmain led 10–6, it wasn't over until Paul McBlane blew the final whistle. It should be noted that the six points Brisbane had on the board were courtesy of a try scored by Tonie Carroll and a goal-kick conversion by their halfback, Ben Walker.

It was a good day to be a Brisbane Broncos fan, because with the game so close to the end, Carroll crashed through Balmain's defence to score a try, which locked the game up at 10–10. With a goal kick still to come, Brisbane could win by converting it, and even though Ben Walker had to take the kick from close to the sideline, as Carroll's try was scored in the left-hand corner of Balmain's in-goal area (the "Latchem" Robinson stand side of Leichhardt Oval), it was their chance to win. The crowd tried "booing" Walker, but his concentration was firm, and he struck the ball sweetly, sending it through the goal posts for the win.

Adam Nable was Balmain's starting hooker for the game, and the team had worked so hard to take it to Brisbane. "I thought we were unlucky…Brisbane always struggled there [Leichhardt Oval], too…we played them there [Leichhardt] a couple of times and it was always a tight game…they [Brisbane] hated playing there" (Nable 2018). Even though they lost, it was a solid performance against a high-calibre club, which showed how competitive Balmain could be.

It would also be the final NRL first-grade game of Steven Price's playing career. Price had made three first-grade appearances for Balmain, but injuries would eventually force him to retire from the game. He was still under twenty-five years old when he turned his attention to coaching. For a decade Price coached lower grades and served in assistant coaching roles at St. George Illawarra, and he was the club's first-grade coach from 2012 to 2014.

Balmain had a fresh challenge ahead of them for Round 12, as they would play for the first time the merged St. George Illawarra Dragons, and making the Illawarra Steelers and St. George Dragons one club gave them an abundant choice of players. Despite some reasonable expectations for their 1999 season, by the conclusion of Round 11, they were eleventh on the competition ladder, and even though Balmain lost to Brisbane, Balmain was still eighth. St. George Illawarra had won five of the eleven games they had played, and by that point of the season, there were some onlookers who questioned the value of that merge, and if it was indeed in the best interest of other clubs to do the same. Home games were split for St. George Illawarra, to represent both sides of their partnership, and Balmain had to travel down to Illawarra's home ground, WIN Stadium, for their Round 12 fixture on Saturday, May 22.

St. George Illawarra completely dominated, winning the game 48–8, and the only Balmain player to crash over their try line was tough front rower Shane Walker. It was his only try for the 1999 season and his second as a Sydney/Balmain Tiger. Walker played with great effort and pride, and losing by such a margin was disappointing. He was the type of player that would do anything to help his team win, which included playing while still recovering from injuries that would have sidelined most other players. St. George Illawarra had too much firepower for Balmain that game. During his career Walker would appear in 178 first-grade games, and he scored five tries. He was a player that had the rare ability to continue to gain further skills as he got older, and in his late twenties, he was one of the form front rowers in the NRL.

St. George Illawarra had every right to smile, with such a convincing win, yet the most remarkable story was the return of Balmain second rower Mark Stimson for that game. Just like former Sydney/Balmain centre William "Bubba" Kennedy, Stimson was another "country hit" that was discovered by Balmain's brilliant network of scouts and recruitment officers who went seeking talent in Country Rugby League (CRL) competitions of New South Wales. Stimson and Kennedy both made their first-grade debuts as Sydney Tigers during Round 1 on Saturday, March 23, 1996, at the Sydney Football Stadium. It was also, of course, the first-grade debut game of lock Glenn Morrison. Balmain played their Round 24 game of the 1998 season on Saturday, August 22, at Leichhardt Oval. It was front rower Paul Sironen's final NRL and farewell game, and the Sydney City Roosters won the game 40–4. Stimson played in the second row for Balmain that game, and he had played each of Balmain's twenty-four games in 1998.

Just three days after Balmain's final game of the 1998 season, Stimson was injured on a plumbing job site at Sydney's Darling Harbour on August 25, when he was buried up to his thighs in rubble after the trench he was working in subsided. He would lose two toes as a result of a slab of concrete pinning his left foot. Losing two toes was enough to potentially end the career of any professional athlete participating in a running/collision sport like rugby league. Recovering from the injury sufficiently to resume the normal activities of living was one thing, but recovering sufficiently to return to playing first-grade rugby league was a completely different challenge. Stimson would play in a modified left boot, and he would appear in ten games for Balmain in 1999.

From the date of the injury on August 25, 1998, it took Stimson 270 days, or eight months and twenty-seven days, to go from a hospital bed, emergency surgery, and then rehabilitation to returning to play first grade in the NRL. His comeback was incredible and inspiring and was by far the most important detail of any game played during Round 12 of the 1999 season. From 1996 to 2000, Stimson made ninety-two first-grade appearances, and some might say the injury significantly contributed to stopping him from reaching two hundred first-grade appearances or more. The fact that he made it back to that level was phenomenal, and he'll always be remembered for his nonstop hard work on the field.

Balmain's Round 12 game against St. George Illawarra was the start of the Dragons' seven-game winning streak, and Balmain were both their first and seventh win of that streak. Some might say that first game against Balmain was the beginning of St. George Illawarra's show of strength, and it was the beginning of their longest winning streak of the season, but their full force as a merged club would be more fully appreciated later in the season.

For Round 13 Balmain faced the North Sydney Bears at North Sydney Oval on Sunday, May 30. The last win North Sydney had had was Round 6 against Balmain. Since then they had been on a six-game losing streak, and they were desperate to try to recover their season with a much-needed win. Adam Nable, who from Round 7 onward had essentially become Balmain's incumbent hooker, recalled, "It's probably one of those games you try to block out [of your memory]," (Nable 2018) because North Sydney won 64–12.

North Sydney would win three more games during the 1999 season, but that day at their home ground, after winning so emphatically, their players shook hands with their fans, and there were some hugs, too. Their players took the opportunity to wave giant North Sydney Bears red-and-black supporter flags affixed to poles to celebrate their win and, in appreciation of their loyal fans that had made the flags, brought them to games and waved them when North Sydney scored points or when rallying the team.

Talk of club mergers was getting louder and louder by Round 13. It was nothing unfamiliar for Balmain because they had been identified as a merge candidate for quite some time, but North Sydney was getting increased attention to amalgamate with another club. There was no indication of a potential partnership between Balmain and North Sydney, yet both clubs could possibly find a respective merge partner. The thought that Balmain had played their last NRL game against North Sydney was a possibility, yet they were both 1908 foundation clubs of the then New South Wales Rugby Football League, and surely ninety-two seasons counted for something, with nearly a century of loyalty and participation from both clubs.

In 1998 North Sydney finished the regular season in fifth place and Manly Warringah in tenth position, which was good enough for both clubs to make the top-ten finals. Geographically, merging both teams would cover Northern Sydney, as they both shared territory borders, but from a fan point of view, partnering those two clubs was equal to sacrilege, as a strong rivalry existed between them. North Sydney was pursuing the path of relocating to Gosford on the New South Wales Central Coast in an effort to stand alone as a club. In 1998 merging the two teams didn't even register in the minds of most loyal fans from both clubs, and in terms of performance, both had played in the 1998 finals, and it was languishing clubs that needed to merge, not them.

How things had changed in less than a year, and by the halfway point of the 1999 season, North Sydney had five wins from the twelve games they had played, and Manly Warringah had three wins from twelve games. North Sydney weren't out of it, though, and a strong second half of the season could turn around their 1999 season and put them in the finals. It didn't happen, of course—North Sydney won three of their twelve games during the second half of the season, finishing fourteenth of seventeen clubs on the competition ladder. Manly Warringah won six games and one draw from their remaining twelve games, but they only finished one place better, at thirteen on the competition ladder.

What fans of those clubs couldn't clearly see was the accumulation of debt, and it was financial weakness that brought the two teams together as the merged Northern Eagles. The club existed from 2000 to 2002, and the Manly Warringah Sea Eagles were reborn in 2003, which was the death of any part of North Sydney at the NRL level. Nobody could have possibly predicted all of that back in Round 13 of the 1999 season, yet it was nevertheless an ending between Balmain and North Sydney as NRL opponents, which history would later reveal as their closing juncture.

Balmain's future was still not fully determined, and even though they had renamed and relocated for their 1995 and 1996 seasons and, since 1997, had been mentioned as a candidate to participate in potential mergers, the mood had got more serious. "It [talk of merging Balmain] didn't really bother me until that 1999 season… it was in all the [news]papers…were we going with Parramatta or Western Suburbs?" was Nable's (2018) recollection of the media scrutiny and pressure placed on Balmain to merge.

By the conclusion of Round 13, Balmain had lost four games in a row, and the latter two were notably heavy losses, so there was a reasonable perception that Balmain needed to get a lot stronger if they were going to have any chance to be competitive in the reduced fourteen-team NRL competition for the year 2000. Another point of view was that Balmain was too weak a club to take that next step, and they potentially faced death at the NRL level.

With the benefit of hindsight, if only Balmain and North Sydney had known the historical significance of their Round 13 game, perhaps the celebrations after the game might have focused more on the ninety-two seasons they had been opponents. Sure, North Sydney deserved to enjoy their big win, yet if players on both teams knew it would be North Sydney lock/second rower Billy Moore's final season in first grade at just twenty-eight years old, there would have been some acknowledgement of him.

Moore was a senior player, but it was common for players to keep playing into their early thirties. He made his first-grade debut during Round 2 on Sunday, March 26, 1989, against Penrith Panthers at their home ground, Penrith Park. He came off the bench for North Sydney, and Penrith won the game 20–0. Moore was a one-club man, and he made 211 first-grade appearances from 1989 to 1999. He was one of the proudest players to wear the maroon jersey of Queensland in State of Origin, and he arguably had some of the most memorable swagger of any Queensland player. His battle cry was to yell, "Queenslander! Queenslander!" as the players walked down the stadium player tunnel and ran out onto the field. He made seventeen appearances for Queensland from 1992 to 1997. Round 13 against Balmain wasn't his final first-grade appearance for North Sydney; he played that during Round 21 on Sunday, July 25, at North Sydney Oval against the Parramatta Eels. He started that game at lock, and Parramatta won the game 44–4. Moore didn't appear in North Sydney's remaining five games of the 1999 season, from Rounds 22 to 26.

If the Balmain players knew Round 13 would be the last time they would line up opposite Billy Moore, there would have been some handshakes and pats on the back for him from some Balmain players, but few if any would have thought for one moment that 1999 would be Moore's final season appearing in first grade. So few players of professional sports get the opportunity to finish on their own terms, and Moore's retirement at twenty-eight years old left his career seeming incomplete for such a warrior of the game. The plethora of combined North Sydney and Manly Warringah players to select from as Northern Eagles, presented limited opportunity for Moore. He could have played on at another club and added value, but he nevertheless chose to conclude his NRL career.

North Sydney winger Brett Dallas had a busy and memorable game against Balmain, scoring four tries, but those would also be his last in the NRL. He was twenty-four years old at the time and still in the prime of his career, having already played for Australia in 1995–96 and for Queensland in State of Origin in 1993 and 1995–97. By the end of the 1999 season, Dallas had made 119 first-grade appearances, and he had scored sixty-four tries, but he would see out his career in the English Super League from 2000 to 2006. He appeared in 177 Super League/Challenge Cup games, with 107 tries.

Front rower Mark O'Meley made his first-grade debut with North Sydney during Round 1 on Sunday afternoon, March 7, 1999, at Parramatta Stadium against Western Suburbs Magpies. He came off the bench for North Sydney, and they won the game 30–12. O'Meley was only seventeen years old at the time—he turned eighteen on May 22. Despite his youth he didn't take a backwards step, lining up against seasoned veterans ten to fifteen years older than him. For the Round 13 game against Balmain, he made his third career start in the front row, and what a career it was, spanning in the NRL 1999–2009, and he played in the English Super League from 2010 to 2013.

As the seasons ticked by during O'Meley's career, he quickly found himself to be one of the last active 1999 North Sydney Bears players. The fact that he started his first-grade career so young added to the longevity of his representation as an enduring North Sydney Bears player. O'Meley did just about everything during his career, which included playing for Australia and New South Wales in State of Origin and a grand final win with the Bulldogs in 2004. He was a no-nonsense, hard-to-stop player, and it all began with the North Sydney Bears.

That Round 13 game would be Balmain front rower Adam Starr and five-eighth Brendan Magnus's final appearance in first grade, with Starr coming off the bench and Magnus starting the game at five-eighth. Neither player could have known it would be their final appearance at that level, as half of the 1999 season still remained, but the future can be cruelly unpredictable. Magnus had made his first-grade debut as a Balmain Tiger coming off the bench during Round 13 on Sunday, June 7, 1998, at Leichhardt Oval. Balmain played Melbourne Storm that afternoon, and Melbourne won the game 25–16. Magnus had good acceleration, and his speed coming off the bench was handy, and he was a good strategist at halfback or five-eighth, but his injection of speed had a way of helping Balmain find gaps in the opposition's defensive line. He appeared in only nine games in 1998, yet he still managed to score three tries.

Round 13 was the final first-grade appearance for some, but for Balmain winger Wade Rothery, it was the beginning. Rothery made his first-grade debut that day, and he had a turn of speed that could bamboozle the opposition, as it was almost like he had springs in his feet, suddenly shifting to his left or right and dancing around a would-be tackler. Once he found some space and got running, Rothery was hard to catch. Given that North Sydney had much of the possession of the ball, Rothery didn't get too many opportunities to show his attacking flair, and he had to do his best to attempt to stop North Sydney's many attacking raids.

Balmain was up against Western Suburbs Magpies for Round 14, and they had started the 1999 season nomadically due to the redevelopment of their home ground, Campbelltown Sports Ground. Western Suburbs had mostly used Parramatta Stadium as a temporary home, but they had also taken a home game to Lathlain Oval in suburban Perth, Western Australia. It was a sunny afternoon when they played Balmain on Sunday, June 6. There were formalities before the game in terms of the official reopening of the venue, along with a few passionate speeches about a hopeful future for Western Suburbs. There were 16,605 spectators in attendance, and Western Suburbs had won a game as recently as Round 12 against Penrith Panthers, which Western Suburbs won 7–6. Balmain's most recent win happened to be their Round 8 game at Leichhardt Oval against Western Suburbs, which Balmain had won 28–16. Suggestions by the media of merging Balmain and Western Suburbs were one thing, but murmurs amongst supporters of both clubs that chats between the executives of the teams had supposedly progressed to more formal discussion added additional importance to the game.

At halftime the game was locked even at 6–6, but late in the second half, a solid tackle on Balmain's five-eighth, Jacin Sinclair, caused him to lose possession of the ball, and Western Suburbs centre Kevin McGuinness swooped on the ball and ran away with it for a try. Western Suburbs won the game 18–12, and they had christened their newly developed home ground with a victory. It would be their final win of the 1999 season and also their last at the NRL level. They would have reasonably anticipated more wins, with still twelve games to go, but alas, there were no more.

Three wins would be it for their 1999 season, leaving them seventeenth on the competition ladder and earning them the unenviable wooden spoon. It was their second consecutive wooden spoon, and in the last twenty years, from 1980 to 1999, they had six last places that all happened during periods of two consecutive seasons, consisting of 1983 and 1984, 1987 and 1988, and 1998 and 1999. Balmain had a wooden spoon season in 1981 and 1994. They were both foundation clubs, and Western Suburbs had won four premierships (1930, 1934, 1948, and 1952), while Balmain had won eleven (1915, 1916, 1917, 1919, 1920, 1924, 1939, 1944, 1946, 1947, and 1969), yet it had been decades since either club had last won one. Both had had their struggles, but when it came to their final meeting in the NRL, the win belonged to Western Suburbs.

On a personal level, the Round 14 game was the first-grade debut of hooker Ben Galea. He came off the bench for Balmain, and he would make one more first-grade appearance during the 1999 season. It was Galea's first season at Balmain; he was twenty years old when he made both appearances, and he would turn twenty-one on August 16. When Galea joined the club and started preseason training in late 1998, there was a perception from some teammates that he was notably confident for a new guy that hadn't yet played a game of first grade. For senior players at the club, this was a bit unexpected, as generally, young new players were somewhat expected to be unassuming in nature and needed to prove themselves.

If Galea came across as overconfident, it was a first impression that wouldn't hold him back, as in subsequent seasons he would become one of the most popular players among his teammates. His NRL career spanned 1999 to 2007, and he played all 152 games as a Tiger. He also played in the English Super League/Challenge Cup from 2008 to 2013, and he had 141 appearances in Super League. In 1999 Galea's confidence might have been misunderstood, which could easily be comparable to a new student at their new school or a new employee at their new company going about their duties confidently as a display of comfort in their new environment. Galea was a versatile player who could cover hooker, five-eighth, second row, and lock.

Round 14 was Michael Ostini's Balmain Tigers first-grade debut. He had made his first-grade debut as a Sydney City Rooster during Round 15 on Sunday, July 14, 1996, against the North Sydney Bears at North Sydney Oval, and Sydney City won the game 30–25. He could play front row or second row, and he had two seasons with South Sydney Rabbitohs from 1997 to 1998 before joining Balmain for the 1999 season. It was a new beginning for Ostini, and he came off the bench for Balmain during Round 14. Conversely, it would be an ending point for five-eighth Jacin Sinclair, as Round 14 would be the final time he appeared in an NRL first-grade game. He would in future years play some first-grade preseason trial games, but Sunday, June 6, 1999, was his last appearance during regular-season play. For Balmain fans it was pleasing that Sinclair had returned to where his career had started, and plenty would say that Balmain was the club where he played his best rugby league.

By the end of Round 14, Balmain was twelfth on the competition ladder, and they still had eleven games left in their regular season. It wasn't an impossible task, but they would need to try and find something extra to attempt to win most of those games and give themselves a chance of perhaps sneaking into the top-eight finals. They had Round 15 off due to the bye, which gave them an extra week to prepare for their Round 16 game against the Penrith Panthers at Leichhardt Oval.

## CHAPTER 8

# BREAKING THE LOSING STREAK— AND STARTING A NEW ONE

It was a sunny afternoon on Sunday, June 20, when Balmain faced Penrith at Leichhardt Oval. Penrith was captained that day by halfback Greg Alexander, and at thirty-four years old, he was a veteran. He had made his first-grade debut coming off the bench for Penrith during their Round 2 game on Wednesday, March 28, 1984, against Manly Warringah at Brookvale Oval. Manly Warringah won easily 26–8, but it was the beginning of a glittering career that would include 265 first-grade appearances. Alexander was Penrith's halfback for the 1991 grand final against the Canberra Raiders, which Penrith won 19–12. It was also the club's maiden grand final win, as well.

He switched clubs after the 1994 season, when he joined new club the Auckland Warriors, and he was their inaugural halfback. He appeared in twenty-one games for them in 1995, which was one short of having played every game of their 1995 season. He'd stay with Auckland for the 1996 season before returning to play for Penrith in the 1997 Super League season. During his career he'd played for Australia and New South Wales. That afternoon at Leichhardt Oval would be the final time Alexander would play a first-grade game against Balmain. He still had some of his magic, and he scored the final try of his first-grade career that afternoon, against Balmain, bringing his total to 111 tries.

There were some hot tempers that day. Exactly why Balmain's lock and captain Darren Senter put a flurry of short jab punches on the face of Penrith front rower Matt Adamson is something only they'll know. Senter had tackled Adamson and had Adamson pinned down, and Senter was on top of Adamson when the punches began. The punches led to an immediate penalty in favour of Penrith. Additionally, Craig Gower was playing five-eighth for Penrith that day, and he wasn't too happy when he made a clean line-break and looked certain to have scored a try, only to have it disallowed as referee Matt Hewitt ruled that the covering tackler had stopped Gower and he had made a double movement at the try line. Gower threw the ball in disgust.

During the second half of the game, Penrith front rower Mark Geyer was sent off. In terms of misconduct, he tried to argue that "it takes two to tango" (as in, he was only retaliating to Balmain players), but Hewitt told Geyer to "Go!" and pointed to the sideline. Geyer took a moment to stare at Hewitt before jogging off the field. The transgression wasn't shocking, such as a head-high tackle that knocked out a Balmain player; it was some heavy contact Geyer made during tackles, but it was enough to break Hewitt's patience.

Geyer had his own history as a Balmain Tiger, having joined the club in 1993, but it was at a time when Geyer was struggling for consistency. His thirteen first-grade appearances with Balmain in 1993 were part of a career that wasn't short of animated moments and, notably, some long suspensions. He had three seasons with the

Western Reds, from 1995 to 1997, and returned back to Penrith in 1998, where he saw out his first-grade career before retiring after the 2000 season. He had his share of achievements, which included the 1991 grand final win, but he would spend ten minutes in the sin bin during that game. He'd played for Australia and New South Wales, too. His confrontation with Queensland captain and five-eighth Wally Lewis during the 1991 State of Origin series had become part of Origin lore.

Despite his complicated career, Geyer had the respect of two Balmain Tiger legends, Steve Roach and Paul Sironen, who publicly expressed their high opinion of Geyer. "I can really relate to him," said Steve Roach in his autobiography (1992, p. 168). "He's a bit like me in that he is emotional on the field and gives the game everything he's got. His enthusiasm and killer instinct have got him into a bit of trouble. But I'd never tell him to quieten down or change his style. If he did that he wouldn't be MG [Mark Geyer] anymore. His benefit to the Panthers, NSW and Australia is his ability to intimidate and take on the opposition. Other players never know just how far Mark is prepared to go. He's one of the best and genuinely colourful players in rugby league." Paul Sironen also made a point of mentioning Geyer in his autobiography: "MG boasts some of the best ball skills you could ever hope to see from a forward. He can throw a great cut-out pass, [and] he can challenge the line" (1997, p. 129). Geyer getting sent off certainly wasn't out of character for him, but at the heart of it was his effort to help Penrith compete against Balmain.

In the end Balmain would win the game 24–16. Amongst Balmain's four try scorers was winger Wade Rothery, and it was the maiden try of his first-grade career. It would also be the only occasion he would play on a winning Balmain first-grade team. For the club, the victory finally brought to an end five straight losses, and they still had ten games left in the season to try to finish as strong as possible.

For Round 17, Balmain flew across to New Zealand to play the Auckland Warriors on Saturday night, June 26, at Ericsson Stadium. Having beaten Auckland during their Round 5 game, Balmain might have liked their chances of another win over them. Since Auckland's inaugural season in 1995, Sydney/Balmain Tigers had played them twice at Ericsson Stadium in Penrose, Auckland, once in 1995 and again in 1998, and they lost both games. Balmain came agonisingly close in 1998, though, with Auckland winning only 21–20. Sydney Tigers had won on New Zealand soil in 1996 when they played their Round 11 home game in New Zealand at the neutral South Island venue Lancaster Park at Phillipstown, Christchurch. A win on the North Island of New Zealand had so far evaded them, and this would be their third meeting at Ericsson. It wasn't Balmain's night, though, as Auckland scored five tries and Balmain wasn't able to get across the try line, with their only points coming from goal kicks. Auckland won easily, 22–4.

For Balmain centre/second rower Justin Yeo, it would be his final first-grade appearance. He came off the bench that game for Balmain, and it was his tenth first-grade appearance of the season. Yeo had turned twenty-two years old on January, 21, 1999, and he had appeared in one first-grade game for North Sydney in 1998, which was also his first-grade debut, during Round 12.

Joining Balmain for the 1999 season was a new opportunity for Yeo. His maiden first-grade team victory occurred when Balmain played Melbourne during Round 2, with Balmain winning 16–6. He had come off the bench for Balmain that game, and he would be part of three more wins as a Balmain Tiger. For many first-grade players, the end is rarely known, and often it becomes realised unceremoniously after the fact. Regardless of everything Yeo might have hoped his NRL career would consist of, no one could take away from him that he made first-grade appearances for two proud foundation clubs. He was a part of North Sydney's and Balmain's club history, which had begun in 1908.

Things weren't getting any easier for Balmain as they travelled north to play Brisbane for their Round 18 game on Sunday, July 4. The last time Balmain had beaten Brisbane was during Round 9 of the 1991 season. The game was played on Sunday, May 19, 1991, at Leichhardt Oval, and Balmain won 14–4. It was also Balmain's first win of the 1991 season. The last time Balmain had beaten Brisbane in Brisbane, though, was Round 3 of the 1989 competition, at the then-named Lang Park. Interestingly, during Brisbane's inaugural season in 1988, Balmain was the first club to beat them. In 1988 they had gone through Rounds 1–6 undefeated, but they took on Balmain for Round 7 at Lang Park on Saturday, April 16, 1988, and Balmain won the game 26–18.

It was ominous that Balmain hadn't had a win over Brisbane at their home ground since 1989. Balmain's wins in 1988 and 1989 were both at Lang Park in Milton, Brisbane, but they were yet to have a win over them at ANZ Stadium in Nathan, Brisbane. It was Balmain's last chance to log a win in Brisbane during the 1990s decade, and it would also be their final opportunity of the twentieth century. Brisbane, though, had other ideas, and they ran away with the game, 42–10.

One highlight for Balmain was second rower Mark Stimson scoring his first try since his return from a potential career-ending injury. It was his only try for the season, and Stimson managed to score at least one try during each season he played first grade from

1996 to 2000.

For twenty-one-year-old front rower Kylie Leuluai, the Round 18 game against Brisbane was his first-grade debut. He came off the bench for Balmain, as he would in another six games for the 1999 season. Leuluai would appear in seventy-eight first-grade games from 1999 to 2006, and he would appear in 261 Super League/Challenge Cup/Super 8s games from 2007 to 2015. He played his entire Super League career for Leeds Rhinos. Leuluai's combined NRL/Super League career would total 339 appearances, and it all began with the Balmain Tigers.

Where one career had just started, another ended, and Round 18 would be the final first-grade appearance of front rower/second rower Michael Ostini. He had made four first-grade appearances for Balmain during the 1999 season. Ostini had spread his career among three foundation clubs: Sydney City (formally Eastern Suburbs), South Sydney, and Balmain. He had made twenty-nine of his thirty-five first-grade appearances with South Sydney and scored his only first-grade career try with them during Round 11 of the 1997 season. Ostini didn't get to play first grade against his former clubs while at Balmain in 1999, and Balmain's Round 19 opponent was South Sydney.

It was Sunday, July 11, at the Sydney Football Stadium when Balmain played South Sydney for their Round 19 game. As far as general rugby league fan and media talk were concerned, both clubs were seen as strugglers in terms of being one of the fourteen clubs to be approved to participate in the rationalised competition for the year 2000. Few loyal fans of either club would dare say it out loud, but there was a reasonable possibility that it might be the final time Balmain and South Sydney played an NRL game as opponents.

Some observers would claim that South Sydney was in a weaker position than Balmain, and during the previous three seasons, they had finished no higher than third-to-last on the ladder. In 1996 South Sydney finished nineteenth of twenty teams, in 1997 they played in the twelve-club ARL competition and finished eleventh, and in 1998 they finished eighteenth of twenty clubs. Sydney Tigers finished twelfth in 1996, Balmain was eighth in 1997, and Balmain finished the 1998 season in thirteenth position.

Going into the 1999 Round 19 game, Balmain was sitting thirteenth on the ladder, and South Sydney was eighth. Balmain had won three of the previous ten games they had played, and they were on a two-game losing streak. South Sydney had won five of their previous ten games played, and they had won their Round 18 game against Penrith, 20–0. Balmain hadn't beaten South Sydney since Round 15 of the 1997 competition, and they had only played each other once in 1998, with South Sydney winning the Round 16 game 16–12.

Tim Brasher was captain and fullback for South Sydney that game in 1998, and it burned the eyes of Balmain fans to see him in South Sydney's primarily cardinal red and myrtle green jersey colours. For the 1999 Round 19 game, Brasher was again South Sydney's starting fullback. He wasn't the only former Tiger on the team, though, as halfback Wes Patten came off the bench for them. Patten had made his first-grade debut as a Balmain Tiger during Round 22 in 1993. He appeared in first grade for the Sydney Tigers in 1995–96, but he joined the Gold Coast Chargers for the 1997 season. Both times Gold Coast played Balmain in 1997, they won, and Patten scored a try in each game.

Balmain still hadn't won an away game during the 1999 season. Things were looking good at halftime, with Balmain ahead 12–0, but South Sydney were phenomenal during the second half, scoring twenty-two unanswered points, and won 22–12. Adam Nable, who played hooker for Balmain that game, said with some frustration (2018), "Maybe we came out a bit confident in the second half... very disappointing...that was a game we should have won."

Despite the loss, the game had a unique detail, as it was the Balmain first-grade debut of five-eighth Nick Shaw. It was also Shaw's final appearance in first grade, and he had turned twenty-one years old only ten days earlier. Interestingly, he had made his first-grade debut as a North Sydney player during Round 7 on April 16 against Sydney City. He came off the bench for North Sydney, and Sydney City won the game 28–16. What made Shaw's first-grade career unique was that he had played two career first-grade games in one season, but one game each for two different clubs.

It was also the final NRL first-grade appearance of Balmain front rower James Gannon, as he came off the bench during the game. Gannon had made his first-grade debut as a Balmain Tiger during Round 1 of the 1998 season. From 1998 to 1999, Gannon made twenty-two first-grade appearances for the club. He managed to gain a release from Balmain during the 1999 season and promptly appeared in the English Super League for Halifax Blue Sox in their Round 20 game on July 28. In the space of seventeen days, he had gone from playing his final NRL game at the Sydney Football Stadium in Moore Park, Sydney, to playing in the Super League at Belle Vue in Wakefield, West Yorkshire, England. Gannon went on to have an impressive Super League career, as he appeared in 225 Super League/Challenge Cup games from 1999 to 2012.

While Balmain's Round 19 loss to South Sydney was disappointing for all seventeen Balmain players that took the field and gave it their best shot, it nevertheless would prove to have its own significance to players and the sport. It would prove to be the final time Balmain and South Sydney met in an NRL game, and while playing for South Sydney from 1998 to 1999, Tim Brasher never lost a game to his former club.

The first time the two clubs met in the New South Wales Rugby Football League was during Round 9 of the inaugural 1908 season on Saturday, July 25, at Birchgrove Oval. Ninety years, eleven months, and sixteen days later, the end had arrived, with their final encounter at the highest club-level of the sport. In 1908 South Sydney won that first game 16–2, and it wasn't until 1911 that Balmain had a win over them, during Round 14 on Saturday, August 26, at Birchgrove Oval. Balmain was ahead 7–0 at halftime, and they went on to win the game 9–3. With so much uncertainty still present by Round 19 of the 1999 season, fans of both clubs could still only hope the future would favour their team. South Sydney, though, were excluded from the fourteen-club competition for the year 2000.

Balmain's Round 20 opponent was St. George Illawarra, and they were in tremendous form, which had silenced some of the critics of merging clubs. They had made a bit of a slow start during their first year as an amalgamated club, but St. George Illawarra had started a six-game winning streak with Balmain back in Round 12. They were eager to make it seven wins in a row as the two clubs met during Round 20. It was Saturday, July 17, at Leichhardt Oval, and St. George Illawarra's seventeen-man lineup was red-hot with talent.

All seven players that made-up their backline had played or would play in the future at representative level, in terms of playing for Australia or State of Origin or both. Nathan Blacklock was their fullback. Mark Coyne was captain, and he and Jamie Ainscough played on each wing. Shaun Timmins and Paul McGregor were the centres pair, and in the halves, Trent Barrett was at halfback and Anthony Mundine was at five-eighth. Winger Rod Wishart had played for Australia and New South Wales in State of Origin, and he came off the bench that day for St. George Illawarra. While St. George Illawarra's forward pack wasn't as decorated in terms of representative experience, lock Craig Fitzgibbon would go on to play for Australia and for New South Wales in State of Origin. Corey Pearson started in the front row for St. George Illawarra that day, and for Balmain fans watching on, it never got any easier seeing Pearson contribute to another club. Craig Hancock played as a centre for Balmain that day, and he was the only Balmain player to have State of Origin representative experience, having played one game for New South Wales in 1995.

All seventeen Balmain players that took part in the game against St. George Illawarra did so not in awe of their opponent, but with all the effort they had. St. George Illawarra won the game 38–16, which made it seven wins in a row, but they would lose the following week to Brisbane, and so their winning streak started and ended with Balmain. The loss compounded a difficult run for Balmain, as they had won one game from their last ten, which was their Round 16 win over Penrith. At a personal level, it would be winger Wade Rothery's final first-grade appearance in the NRL. His first-grade career had therefore begun and ended as a Balmain Tiger, with seven appearances, but he did manage to score one of Balmain's three tries against St. George Illawarra.

The dominant performance by St. George Illawarra certainly added some currency to what amalgamating clubs could offer. Given Balmain's one win from the previous ten games, those looking at Balmain as a prime candidate for a merger could reasonably argue that at the very least it would achieve a strengthening of resources.

Whatever noise the media and fans of the sport made about Balmain's potential future, they still had six games left in the season, and that's what the team would be focused on. Their Round 21 opponent was Newcastle at Leichhardt Oval, and it was a fresh chance to end their losing streak.

# CHAPTER 9

# PLAYING FOR PRIDE AND MAKING THE BIGGEST DECISION

It was a cold Sydney winter night on Saturday, July 24, when Balmain took on Newcastle for their Round 21 game. Their most recent win over them was as Sydney Tigers during Round 4 of the 1996 season at Marathon Stadium, with the Tigers winning 24–12. Even though they had returned to be Balmain Tigers for the 1997 season, Newcastle had a comfortable record at Leichhardt Oval, having won their Round 11 (1997) game there 26–18, as well as their Round 23 game in 1998, winning it 30–16.

The 1998 game was particularly memorable because it was played in wet, muddy conditions on Sunday afternoon, August 16. Rain had caused some puddles of water on some areas of the playing surface, which meant that when players were tackled, there was a splash of water as they made contact with the ground. The mud and water caused some havoc when it came to handling the ball, and the ball was unpredictable, as a kicked ball might skid along the slippery surface of the ground or abruptly stop when it rolled into a puddle of water.

Probably one of the strangest sights, though, was seeing New-castle player Danny Buderus start the game at fullback. Buderus had been coming off the bench exclusively until Round 21 in 1998, when he made his maiden first-grade run-on start at hooker against Illawarra. During the next three rounds, he started at either fullback or centre, which would become uncharacteristic positions for him, as he played the vast majority of his first-grade career at hooker. His career would span 1997–2013 (from 2009 to 2011, he made eighty-two Super League/Challenge Cup appearances for Leeds Rhinos), with 257 ARL/NRL first-grade appearances. Playing hooker took him to the heights of playing for New South Wales and Australia. Only twice would he start an NRL first-grade game at fullback, and the final time at first-grade level was against Balmain during Round 23 in 1998.

When Balmain met Newcastle for their Round 21 game in 1999, Buderus was their starting hooker. Newcastle's halfback, An-drew Johns, didn't play that game, but they still had some high-qual-ity players take the field, with Robbie O'Davis, Jason Moodie, Mat-thew Gidley, Mark Hughes, Timana Tahu, and Matthew Johns. All of those players had or would play at State of Origin level, with O'Davis playing for Queensland and the rest all playing for New South Wales. There was no doubt, though, that the absence of An-drew Johns was a plus for Balmain, because as halfback he coordi-nated so much of Newcastle's attack and directed the team around the field. Justin Holbrook started at halfback with the absence of Johns, and it would be Holbrook's third first-grade appearance of his NRL career. Balmain had caught a bit of a break, as Andrew Johns was already considered one of the sport's best active players.

Newcastle's forward pack had gone through some transition, though. Front rower Paul Rauhihi had made his first-grade debut during Round 17, and the game against Balmain was his fourth career game, but it would be his maiden run-on start. He would go on to be an enforcer and a very hard man to stop when he got a run-on, but his time at Newcastle would end after the 2000 season, and he joined the Bulldogs for the 2001 season. In 1999 Rauhihi was a good player, but he would become a feared and an even better player as his career progressed. Newcastle icon and front rower Paul Harragon had made his final first-grade appearance during Round 11, but his retirement was still pending, despite his not taking the field to play Balmain. Harragon was a rare one-club player, and interestingly, his first-grade debut was against Balmain during Round 18 on Sunday, July 17, 1988, at Leichhardt Oval. He came off the bench, and Balmain won the game 18–16.

Balmain didn't have to lock horns with Harragon, as the clubs were only scheduled to meet once in 1999, and with Harragon out of action, the only player from Newcastle's starting forward pack from the 1997 ARL grand final winning team was Bill Peden, and he was starting the game at lock against Balmain. Newcastle grand final front rower Tony Butterfield was unavailable for the Balmain game, and second rowers Wayne Richards and Adam Muir were playing for other clubs in 1999. Grand final lock Marc Glanville was playing in the Super League for English club Leeds Rhinos. Not to take anything away from the talents of the forwards Newcastle had in 1999, but it was fair to say their 1997 counterparts were a special group.

Even with the changes to Newcastle's personnel, they were having a reasonable season, and going into their game against Balmain they were on a six-game winning streak, and they had won eight of their ten previous games. They were third on the competition ladder going into Round 21. Balmain were trying to break their own four-game losing streak, and having won just one out of their last ten games, they were in fourteenth position on the competition ladder going into the game. Many experts and onlookers reasonably thought Newcastle's fixture with Balmain would make it seven wins in a row for them.

The pressure to win was on all of Balmain's players, but for winger Mark Luland, Round 21 in 1999 was his first-grade debut. Newcastle's backline had plenty of skill and pace to it, but Luland was essentially unknown to them, and thinking of Newcastle the same way would help minimise any distractions for him. It was a cold night, but at least there wasn't incessant rain and puddles of water on the playing surface.

The end score suggested a close game, with Balmain surprising plenty with their 20–16 win, but Balmain contained Newcastle throughout the game, and it was Newcastle that was on the back foot, playing catch-up with Balmain when it came to scoring. Both clubs scored an equal number of tries, with three each, but fullback Joel Caine had a perfect night for Balmain, successfully kicking all four of his goal kicks. Halfback Justin Holbrook had the goal-kicking duties for Newcastle, and he had a bit of a tough night, kicking through only two of the five attempts he made.

The win was pleasing for Balmain, but it came at a cost, as it would be Ben Duckworth's final game of the 1999 season. He had started the game as a second rower, but injury brought an early end to his season. He was limited to eleven first-grade appearances in 1999 due to the injury. In 1998, his season also came to a premature end due to injury, and Round 18 was his final game that season. He had appeared in all eighteen games up until that point in 1998 but missed the remaining six games. Ironically, Balmain's final win of the 1998 season was Round 18, with their 18–0 win over North

Queensland at Leichhardt Oval. Duckworth would miss Balmain's remaining five games of the 1999 season, and coincidentally, he had again sustained a season-ending injury in a game Balmain had won. Duckworth's creativity would be missed. For Mark Luland, though, his NRL first-grade career had begun with a team win, and that was something to enjoy. The result lifted Balmain one spot up the ladder to thirteenth, and it ended Newcastle's two-game winning streak at Leichhardt Oval.

Balmain had an incredibly big week ahead of them, as members of Balmain Tigers Football Club would vote on merging with the Western Suburbs Magpies, and their (Western Suburbs) football club members would likewise vote on the evening of July 27 at their respective leagues' clubs. Balmain had played Newcastle three days earlier and won the game, but the club's future for the 2000 season and beyond would be decided with five games still to be played of the 1999 season.

On July 15, Balmain's board had met and decided it would focus solely on a potential amalgamation with Western Suburbs. Up until that point, Parramatta was still on the shortlist as a possible partner for Balmain, but they were a strong club with plenty of money and weren't in any great need of merging with another club. There was a perception among some Balmain supporters that any relationship with Parramatta would be a takeover by Parramatta, and Balmain would be left with little to no say, and Balmain's identity could easily be lost. Fans of the club were only speculating with such assertions, but there was no doubt Parramatta would have expanded its territorial borders by gaining Balmain.

Some onlookers took the critical view that trying to merge Balmain and Western Suburbs put two weaker clubs together, and they questioned if the merge could have long-term success. Balmain had established good early dialogue with Western Suburbs, but Balmain had very specific reasons for considering a partnership with another club. Balmain CEO Danny Munk recalls,

> [Merging with Western Suburbs Magpies] was the one that grew legs and grew legs very quickly...[At the start of 1999] it was active because the board needed to really understand where things were going to be...We knew the state of Leichhardt Oval [and] what was required for it...we knew already that if they [the NRL] wanted to test us against the stadium at Parramatta or what the Broncos had or Townsville had or what the Storm had...we couldn't compete...our problem was... even though Leichhardt [Municipal] Council were saying very supportive things, they weren't really financially supporting Leichhardt Oval...Balmain had to wear the costs for most of the maintenance and the running of the oval. Even though we got support from the management of Leichhardt Council...Leichhardt Council itself didn't want to put capital into the ground, so we knew what our risks were at Leichhardt Oval.
>
> We also knew financially...we had the casino [Sydney Harbour Casino/Star City] that had opened, and all the [local] pubs had got poker machines over the previous ten years...we were in a situation where we probably had some of the most intense competition in the whole Sydney market with regards to casinos, pubs and clubs...we were in constant competition...My concern was we

could probably afford to put a team together for the year 2000, but to be able to put a team together that had twenty-five elite players plus another group of players behind that to play in the lower levels that had the potential to play first grade, we were going to struggle…Our biggest risk was getting into the competition [for the year 2000 onward] as a standalone team, and how we were going to fund it…One of the things that did occur, and it was very obvious by the way the NRL was running it, that the cost of football was going to escalate…That's where it became very difficult for a lot of clubs (Munk 2018).

Rumours had caused some confusion for Balmain Tigers supporters and members of the football club well prior to the 1999 season. The Sydney Tigers venture had lasted two years, and since returning to Balmain Tigers in 1997, the club had been mixed and matched in numerous scenarios, and the chatter from outside the club seemed to lack focus on Balmain standing alone. Munk knew it was essential to put people on the right page, and the July 27 special general meeting was a chance to objectively consider all the available facts. According to Munk,

We needed to supply information to the [football club] members…there was a lot of misinformation out there…The Tigers have got a lot of money, don't you worry we can standalone, we don't need to do this we don't need to do that. The NRL wouldn't do that to the Tigers blah, blah. The reality was the NRL was focused on reducing teams and whoever it took out of play it took out of play…So we had to supply a lot of information to the members…A lot of our membership did not want to hear that the world around them was going to change. They'd grown up with Balmain…people in the area hated the very concept that the structure of Balmain Tigers was going to change…it wasn't a case that the board didn't feel the same…we had people on our board who were 'black and gold' from the day they were born… you had the likes of John Chalk who lived and breathed in Balmain…you couldn't think of anyone more black and gold than Chalky…on the same hand, he had a business head…you had a lot of people on our board who were just as passionate or more passionate than the supporters. These were people who believed in black and gold…at the meeting when we were looking at joining up with Western Suburbs, some of the people who lived and breathed Balmain all their lives like Steve Roach, Keith Barnes, and Wayne Pearce they didn't get up there and say we think this is a great idea we'd love to do it, they said this is what we have to do otherwise we're going to lose what we've got…I know in the case of Keith [Barnes] it nearly broke his heart…Keith is a man with enough courage to say, it may not be what I like but it's what we need to do (Munk 2018).

Participation in the 2000 NRL season was subject to a criteria assessment designed by the NRL, and the NRL would evaluate clubs based on several measurements. This included how many junior clubs/number of participants were within the club's respective catchment areas/junior leagues, sponsorship arrangements and how much money they provided, and home and away crowd numbers based on the 1995, 1996, and 1998 seasons. Crowds for the 1997 season were not considered because of the split ARL and Super League competitions. Gate income and the profitability of the leagues club were also gauges, and on-field performance was measured by the NRL. The NRL would then rank the clubs based on the criteria and decide the fourteen highest-ranked clubs to be licensed to participate in the 2000 season. Munk's recollection of the criteria process was that

> [it was] a fairly detailed assessment of your business...so it looked at the financial viability of the organisation...it looked at your revenue opportunities...it looked at what was going to be the structure of your teams and your members... it looked at what your sponsorship levels were... what were the full costs of running your team...it looked at what your merchandise was...what your ticketing was...it looked at your facilities [and all related facilities]...what was your administration structure...what were you investing in junior league...there was a whole range of items so the NRL could get a true assessment of your viability.
>
> Out of the seventeen teams fourteen would be kept...unless of course you went into a joint venture where you were guaranteed a position... that was a strategy by the NRL...St. George and Illawarra went into a joint venture, and they automatically locked up one spot...that put the pres-

sure on everyone else because you were no longer competing for fourteen spots [leaving thirteen licences]…so that meant other clubs were in a situation where if you even felt that you weren't going to make the criteria, you were now at risk because the position regarding your future was no longer in your hands, [the decision] was going to be made by someone else…that's what also put pressure on going into joint ventures…A number of clubs made the decision that the best way going forward to be parties of controlling our destiny was as joint venture clubs (Munk 2018).

The NRL would publicly announce its criteria findings on October 15, 1999; therefore, Balmain and Western Suburbs were giving themselves an opportunity to decide their own futures before then with their respective special general meetings on July 27. Members of both clubs would have the choice to vote to stand alone as a club, or they could vote for a new entity, which would be uniting Balmain and Western Suburbs as a merged club. There was a concern among many supporters of both clubs to "merge or die," and Munk was very aware of this. Looking back on the mood at that time, he recalls,

It certainly created a stress point, no question about that, because the NRL wasn't really giving you many options if you didn't become part of the competition…They weren't offering a quality second-tier competition…so it was really a case that you are either involved with the NRL or you're in the backblocks…financially being in the backblocks is in some ways a positive thing because the cost of running football becomes minimal…the money going into football is reasonably proportional to what the business can afford because the competitions aren't that intensive…the problem is at NRL level there are some clubs that can't put in unlimited funds (Munk 2018).

By the night of the special general meeting, members of both clubs had some appreciation that combining resources as a merged club was the most secure direction for the clubs, and they certainly made that known, with the vote overwhelmingly in favour of the merge. Balmain members voted 295 (for the merge) to nine (to stand alone), and Western Suburbs members voted 254 to seven in resounding support of the merge. Two 1908 foundation clubs had thus decided to become one and so would begin the process of formalising the joint venture with the NRL.

Interestingly, the combined number of voting members from both clubs was not even one thousand people, and there were tens of thousands of Balmain Tigers and Western Suburbs supporters. At a time when the internet was still in its infancy, an online poll may have captured the view of many more people, and such data could have complemented the decision-making process. To some fans of both clubs, it seemed that such a huge decision was made by such a small number of people. It is reasonable to think that, had the proposed merger taken place a decade later, with internet usage and social media having made considerable progress by then, more online polls could have been used as further points of reference to complement the votes of members.

It seemed that other stakeholders of the clubs weren't eligible voting members, such as season ticketholders that may not have had a football club membership, as well as those football club members that hadn't yet qualified to vote and the legion of fans of both clubs who didn't get to have their say. A comprehensive fan-based vote was missing, yet time was elapsing quickly, with five rounds left in the 1999 season and eighty days until October 15, when the NRL would announce its criteria assessment findings. It would have been a nice touch to engage fans of both clubs with a fan vote, yet time was so precious, and the sooner Balmain and Western Suburbs made a decision, the quicker their future would be formalised.

The football club's member votes nevertheless confirmed the consensus that merging both teams was the most secure long-term pathway to retaining the identity of both clubs within a new entity, that being the Wests Tigers. It didn't mean there were hugs and celebration, but rather, there was a big job ahead in terms of constructing the new club while seeing out the rest of Balmain's and Western Suburbs' 1999 season.

Four days after the special general meeting vote, Balmain was back at Leichhardt Oval, playing their Round 22 game against the Sydney City Roosters. Saturday night, July 31, was eerie, as the Balmain Tigers (as a first-grade NRL club) had now begun their journey towards the ending, and Sydney City went into the game as firm favourites, sitting second on the competition ladder. It was another cold night, and with just 7,733 people in attendance, the sparseness at Leichhardt Oval added to what had been a week of mixed emotions.

At an individual level, there were beginnings and endings that occurred during the Round 22 game against Sydney City for some Balmain players. Coming off the bench, second rower Luke O'Donnell made his first-grade debut, and at eighteen years old he was predicted to be a player with a bright future. O'Donnell would go on to make 188 first-grade appearances, and he made twenty-seven appearances in the English Super League/Challenge Cup with Huddersfield Giants. He reached representative levels of the game playing for Australia, NRL All Stars, and New South Wales. The end of his NRL career would have a link to the beginning, as he would finish playing with (the slightly renamed) Sydney Roosters. He came off the bench for Sydney during the 2013 NRL grand final, and they won the game 26–18.

To end on such a high point was the type of career finish players dreamed of, but the pathway wasn't easy for O'Donnell, and on that cold Saturday night when he made his first-grade debut in 1999, he was sin-binned. His infraction wasn't malicious; it was a situation where Sydney City had some momentum and was getting closer to Balmain's try line, and O'Donnell was attempting to reduce their pace by making a slow-to-rise floppy tackle. Referee Paul Simpkins didn't like what he saw, and O'Donnell was sent from the field. As the years went on, O'Donnell would become the last Balmain Tigers first-grade player to appear in the NRL. Being eighteen years old when he made his first-grade debut and finishing his career at thirty-two meant he was the final first-grade flag-bearer of the proud foundation club Balmain Tigers. Coming off the bench for each game, O'Donnell would make three first-grade appearances as a Balmain Tiger, which included their final game in the NRL during Round 26 against the Canberra Raiders.

O'Donnell's sin-binning during his first-grade debut game had minimal impact on the result, as Sydney City had a good hold on their final NRL first-grade game against Balmain, winning comfortably 22–10. Balmain were restricted to one try, with five-eighth James Webster scoring his maiden try in first grade, and Sydney City had got over Balmain's try line four times. On paper Sydney City had a lot of talent, with the likes of Richie Barnett, Jack Else-good, Matt Sing, Ivan Cleary, Shannon Hegarty, Brad Fittler, Adrian Lam, Quentin Pongia, Bryan Fletcher, David Barnhill, and Luke Ricketson, and they were always going to be a challenging opponent for Balmain.

One of Sydney City's players that came off the bench for them was former Balmain Tiger utility Nathan Wood. Wood had made his first-grade debut as a Balmain Tiger during Round 17 on Saturday, July 24, 1993, coming off the bench. The game was played at Leichhardt Oval against the St. George Dragons, and St. George snuck away with the win 18–16. Wood would stay with Balmain through the 1994 season, and in total he made nineteen first-grade appearances as a Balmain Tiger before joining Sydney City for the 1995 season. Wood's younger brother Garth joined Balmain for the 1999 season, but Garth wasn't on Balmain's first-grade team for the Round 22 game, and they didn't get an opportunity to play against each other in first grade during the 1999 season.

The Round 22 game was the final NRL game for Balmain centre Jason Webber. He had made his first-grade debut as a Balmain Tiger during Round 3 on Saturday, March 22, 1997, at Carrara in Queensland against the Gold Coast Chargers, coming off the bench. Gold Coast won the game 26–6, but at twenty-four years old, Webber had broken through at the first-grade level. By rugby league standards, that age made Webber a bit of a mature first-grade debutant, yet Balmain was a club that went in search of players that needed the right opportunity and whose talents might not have been fully appreciated by other clubs.

Balmain had a notable record of finding underestimated players, and Mark Stimson and William Kennedy proved that there were capable players out there that were a bit older who just needed the right opportunity. Webber was much the same, and when it came to discovering and signing such players, Danny Munk fondly recalls some of the layers involved in the process: "You had guys like John Chalk…and a lot of past players that acted as scouts… my skill was signing the contract at the end of it…my role was to make sure there was funding there for it…the accolades of getting some of the players that relates to guys like the John Chalks, the networks that he created through long-term relationships…Keith [Barnes] knew what a player wanted and he knew how to package it together…I learnt quite a bit from John Chalk, Neil Whittaker, and Keith Barnes" (Munk 2018).

Webber was another good find, as his firm tackling skills could bring a player to a sudden halt. He played his entire ARL/NRL career as a Balmain Tiger, from 1997 to 1999, appearing in fifty-two first-grade games, and he scored fourteen tries for the club. Injury brought Webber's 1999 season to a premature end. Certainly, he would have very much liked to have been on the field when his younger brother Nathan made his first-grade debut as a Balmain Tiger during Balmain's Round 26 game against the Canberra Raiders, which was Balmain's final NRL game. It's possible both Webber brothers might have played alongside each other in the centres or at least shared the field together were it not for Jason's injury.

Jason's rugby league career continued in the English Super League, as he joined Salford City Reds for the 2000 season. He would go on to make thirty-one appearances in Super League/Challenge Cup. Finishing the 1999 season at Round 22 was frustrating for Jason, yet he nevertheless completed his NRL career at Leichhardt Oval, playing against another 1908 foundation club. For Balmain it was also the final first-grade NRL game they would play against a fellow foundation club.

The team had four games left as NRL Balmain Tigers, and

Round 23 was against Manly Warringah at Brookvale Oval. Several Balmain players had their own links to Manly Warringah, but now that Balmain was committed to merging with Western Suburbs, the amalgamation vultures were keen to peck away at Manly Warringah and North Sydney. With Balmain assured a future as Wests Tigers, the "merge or die" pressure was now on Manly Warringah, but that could make them an unpredictable opponent for Balmain.

It was Sunday, August 8, and for Round 23 Manly Warringah assembled a team with plenty of quality players from their high-flying days, such as Terry Hill, John Hopoate, Nik Kosef, Cliff Lyons, Jim Serdaris, Neil Tierney, Steve Menzies, Owen Cunningham, and Daniel Gartner. Manly Warringah had won the 1996 grand final, and so many players from that team were on the ground that afternoon, yet they sat in twelfth place on the competition ladder going into their game against Balmain, and Balmain was right behind them, still sitting at thirteenth despite their Round 22 loss to Sydney City. Considering that Manly Warringah also played in the 1997 ARL grand final, to think that nearly two seasons later they were being encouraged to merge with North Sydney seemed almost unbelievable. Had things gone downhill that badly for Manly Warringah in just under two years, or was it just convenient to pair them with North Sydney? These were both questions that supporters of each club and the sport never received a comprehensive answer to.

There was so much speculation about their future swirling in the air that not even Manly Warringah's Sea Eagles could fly above it all, yet they still had to continue on with their remaining four games of the 1999 season. It was nearly impossible for Manly Warringah to reach the top-eight finals, and even if they won their final four games, they still wouldn't be able to break even with wins and losses. Even then (breaking-even), they would need other results to go their way, therefore Manly Warringah was playing for pride but perhaps a very slim chance of making the finals. Despite only losing one of their remaining four games, two wins and a draw meant they finished the 1999 season in thirteenth place. Reaching the finals might have kept some of the amalgamation vultures away, and had Manly Warringah not lost seven consecutive games to start the 1999 season, they may well have found a spot in the finals. Balmain could take a small amount of confidence knowing they had already beaten Manly Warringah during the 1999 season, and they were the seventh club to defeat them during their seven straight losses.

For their Round 23 game, Balmain's focus was winning for pride and the legacy of the club. Balmain had its share of players on the ground that afternoon who had called Manly Warringah home, which included fullback Shannon Nevin, winger Craig Hancock, halfback Craig Field, and hooker Adam Nable. What none of them knew at the time was that it would be the final first-grade game they would play against Manly Warringah and the final first-grade game they would play at Brookvale Oval. The significance of the occasion at a personal level was a more notable recollection for Balmain players than the final score, as Manly Warringah ran away with the game, winning 44–14.

The Round 23 game was Shannon Nevin's final appearance in first grade, yet his connection to Manly Warringah was profound. He had made his first-grade debut for Manly Warringah during Round 1 on Sunday, March 12, 1995, against South Sydney at the Sydney Football Stadium. He came off the bench that game. His last first-grade game for Manly Warringah was the 1997 ARL grand final on Sunday, September 28, against Newcastle. He scored his last first-grade try during the grand final, which Newcastle won inspiringly, 22–16.

Having also played lower grades for Manly Warringah and spending a significant portion of his life living in their territory on Sydney's Northern Beaches, he never wanted to leave the club, but joining Balmain for the 1998 season was a better opportunity to progress his career. He had made twenty-nine first-grade appearances for Manly Warringah from 1995 to 1997, and his thirty-first and final first-grade appearance for Balmain had taken him back to his beginnings. Nevin couldn't have known that it would be his final first-grade appearance at just twenty-three years old, with so much potential career ahead of him, yet time would confirm that Sunday afternoon as his final first-grade game. Starting the game at fullback, he got to wear the number-one jersey in first grade for the final time and as a Balmain Tiger. He was part of Balmain's history, and he appeared in more first-grade games (thirty-one) during his two seasons at Balmain than in the three previous years at Manly Warringah (twenty-nine games).

It was also the final first-grade appearance of Brad Smith, as he came off the bench for Balmain. He was at his best playing second row, and he appeared in eleven first-grade games for Balmain during the 1999 season. With his having appeared in twenty-seven first-grade games for St. George from 1995 to 1998, his season at Balmain brought his total to thirty-eight first-grade appearances. Perhaps it was unlucky that, when it came to Smith's first-grade career, two years in a row (1998 and 1999) he played for clubs that would form part of mergers.

Despite the rumours, by the end of Round 23, the idea of a joint venture between North Sydney and Manly Warringah still seemed inconceivable, at least from the point of view of fans of the sport. The amalgamation vultures, though, would eventually get their way, and the two clubs would merge to become the Northern Eagles. Two clubs that passionately disliked each other were always going to be a stepfamily at best, but the NRL criteria findings publicly announced on October 15 confirmed what most fans of the game already knew, which was that Manly Warringah could have stood alone, as they finished ranked eleventh based on the criteria, and North Sydney was placed fourteenth. With St. George Illawarra guaranteed one of the fourteen licences to participate in the 2000 NRL season, that left only thirteen, yet Manly Warringah were good for their own licence, with the criteria determining them in eleventh position. It didn't matter, though, as Manly Warringah was committed to the merger. From 2000 to 2002, the Northern Eagles club spluttered along, but it would collapse and Manly Warringah would return for the 2003 NRL season.

With their resounding win over Balmain during Round 23, Manly Warringah did finish the 1999 season looking more like their high-flying selves of past seasons, despite not qualifying for the top-eight finals. The indicators, though, were more about their performance against opponents. For Round 24 they had a 26–26 draw against Brisbane, who had won both the 1998 minor premiership and grand final. Brisbane would also finish in eighth place to qualify for the 1999 finals. In Round 25 they took on South Sydney and won 18–2, and for their final game of the season, they played St. George Illawarra during Round 26, with St. George Illawarra edging them out to win 20–18. Finishing in sixth place, St. George Illawarra would progress through the finals to reach the 1999 NRL grand final.

Balmain's final three games of the 1999 season would first return them to Leichhardt Oval to play Parramatta, which would be followed by two away games. As it was Balmain's home farewell game, it would be a significant occasion. Parramatta, though, were riding high in first place on the competition ladder, where they had sat for the two previous weeks. Balmain's most recent win over Parramatta had been during Round 21 on Friday night, August 22, 1997, at Leichhardt Oval. Balmain won 26–6, and there were 18,203 people in attendance at the game. Round 24 on Saturday night, August 14, 1999, was nearly two years after that wonderful win, and Balmain fans would hope with all their hearts that it would somehow be their night to positively remember.

# CHAPTER 10

# BALMAIN'S FINAL THREE NRL GAMES—AND WHAT FOLLOWED

There was rain on August 14, 1999, and with more expected during the evening, it meant some Balmain Tigers supporters weren't quite prepared to brave the weather to see Balmain's final NRL game at Leichhardt Oval for Round 24. At the ground's entry gates, spectators received a souvenir A4-sized cardboard print, coloured with a gentle orange background and firmer black and orange for its title and words. Also marking the occasion on the print were pictures of Balmain legends. The words were

> Celebrate the Last Farewell
> Leichhardt Oval
> The end of an era 1908–1999
> *I was at Leichhardt Oval to celebrate the*
> *"End of a Great Era"*
> The Last Farewell of the Balmain Tigers versus
> Parramatta Eels
> Saturday 14 August 1999

Had it not been for the weather, twenty thousand spectators would have crammed into Leichhardt Oval, but 15,230 attended the game despite the inclement conditions. Adam Nable was Balmain's starting hooker, and as the game got under way, the weather became worse. "I remember it was pouring with rain and it was cold…but to be part of that history was great," said Nable (2018). Joel Caine was Balmain's fullback that game, and he recalled, "I was pleased to score a try in that game…it was probably the worst conditions I've played in [cold with heavy rain]…Laurie Nichols was out there [close to the sideline of the ground] in his singlet, it's pouring down with rain…I think of him, that's what I remember most" (Caine 2018).

Nichols was regarded as perhaps rugby league's most dedicated fan, and his team was the Balmain Tigers. He defied decades of forgettable fashions, such as the 1980s, by most often having the same hairstyle and choice of clothing. His near-buzz cut, snowy grey head of hair and a Balmain Tigers singlet, regardless of the winter temperatures, with dark or black denim jeans or trousers was his usual game-day uniform. He'd shadowbox on the sidelines of the grounds, punching away at the air in support of Balmain/Sydney Tigers. He'd get the Balmain crowd going with his energy and war cries, plus he had so many great rhymes. "Wayne Pearce. He's so fierce," and "Garry Jack. World's best back," were just a couple. He was pushing eighty years old, yet his passion for Balmain was impossible to match, and he had covered several decades during good and bad times for the club.

It was interesting that Caine's highlight was the dedication of Nichols, because despite a flat-out effort by all the Balmain players that night in the soaking wet, it was Caine that contributed the most points, much to the delight of the shadowboxing Nichols.

When it came to goal-kicking, Caine booted successfully each of his four attempts, and his try was a bit awkward, with Parramatta fullback Chris Quinn's attempted tackle keeping Caine on his back as he dived over Parramatta's try line, but Caine managed to shift the ball from one arm to the other, and he managed to place the ball down on the saturated grass for a try.

The game had additional personal significance for Balmain winger Mark Luland, as he scored his maiden and only NRL first-grade try that game. It would also be the final game of his NRL career, with Luland making all four of his first-grade appearances for Balmain during their 1999 season.

Halfback Craig Field had contributed to the scoring, too, and even though Parramatta was tipped to win the game as hot favourites, at halftime Balmain led 8–4, and at fulltime they won 20–10. It was a sweet final home win for Balmain, and the loss was costly for Parramatta because they would finish one win behind 1999 minor premiers Cronulla-Sutherland. Had Parramatta won the game by a considerable margin, they would have been minor premiers.

Leichhardt Oval home farewells for stalwart Balmain players had had some disappointments in the past. Wayne Pearce's farewell game at Leichhardt Oval was Round 21 on Sunday, August 19, 1990. Coincidentally, Balmain's opponent was the Parramatta Eels, and 14,943 people attended the game to say goodbye to Pearce on home soil. Parramatta, though, snuck away with the win, 14–10.

The final home game of Garry Jack, Steve Roach, and David Brooks was Round 21 on Sunday, August 23, 1992. Balmain played St. George that day, with 17,365 spectators watching on, and St. George got away with the win, 20–14. Garry Jack would make a comeback as a Sydney Tiger, but that Sunday in 1992 was his final first-grade appearance at Leichhardt Oval. Jack, Roach, and

Brooks had contributed significantly to Balmain's boom decade of the 1980s, but alas, their final game at Leichhardt Oval was a narrow loss.

Ben Elias played his last first-grade game there during Round 21 on Sunday, August 21, 1994. The Tigers' opponent, Penrith Panthers, won that game 22–10, and 7,810 spectators were there to see his last game, as well as what was expected to be Balmain's last game at Leichhardt Oval, as they would be Sydney Tigers for the 1995–96 seasons, with Parramatta Stadium their home ground.

Paul Sironen's final game as a Balmain Tiger was at home during Round 24 on Saturday night, August 22, 1998. It seemed that rain liked to fall during Round 24 at Leichhardt Oval, but it was nothing like the same round in 1999. Sydney City Roosters won Sironen's final game comfortably, 40-4, and it seemed that Leichhardt Oval farewells had a losing streak that needed to be broken.

Despite the loss during Round 24 in 1998, talk amongst those running the club and chat from fans was optimistic about Balmain's future as a standalone club, yet much had changed in the space of nearly a full year. Balmain's Round 24 game of the 1999 season had achieved what numerous other Leichhardt Oval farewells had been unable to achieve, which was a win. That final home victory over Parramatta was for all past and present players and coaches, and also for all past and present stakeholders of the club, which included all Balmain Tigers fans. It may have been a saturating night, but the win dried much of the cold, and the victory helped somewhat calm the reality that there would be no Balmain Tigers club playing in the NRL from the year 2000.

Round 24, though, wasn't the end of Balmain's 1999 season, as they still had two away games to complete their year. It began with their Round 25 game against the Canterbury-Bankstown Bulldogs at Stadium Australia. There was plenty of history between the two clubs, but during the 1980s Canterbury-Bankstown had a perfect record against Balmain in finals play. It started with their 1985 qualifying finals win, 14–8, and in 1986 they played the preliminary final game, with Canterbury-Bankstown winning it 28–16. That loss cost Balmain a spot in the 1986 grand final. Then there was the 1988 grand final, which was Balmain's first appearance in a grand final since 1969, and Canterbury-Bankstown won the game 24–12.

The 1980s had been Balmain's last big decade, and ten years later Balmain was playing Canterbury-Bankstown for the last time in an NRL game. By Round 25 of 1999, the only links to the 1988 grand final that night was in the coaching booths of the respective teams. Coach Wayne Pearce was Balmain's lock and captain in the 1988 grand final, and Canterbury-Bankstown's coach, Steve Folkes, played second row for them in the grand final.

Even though there were no Balmain or Canterbury-Bankstown players on the field for the Round 25 game who had played in the 1988 grand final, Balmain played the 1989 grand final against the Canberra Raiders, and Canterbury-Bankstown had recruited halfback Ricky Stuart and lock/second rower Bradley Clyde from Canberra following the 1998 season. Canberra (much to the heartache of Balmain's players and all the fans of the club) won the 1989 grand final in extra time 19–14, and Clyde was awarded the Clive Churchill Medal as "man of the match." Both players took the field for Canterbury-Bankstown for the Round 25 game, with Stuart at halfback and Clyde in the second row. So much had changed in just over a decade since 1988, and there had been a reasonable assumption that Stuart and Clyde would be one-club Canberra players, but both players would finish their first-grade careers with two seasons at Canterbury-Bankstown from 1999 to 2000.

In 1988 and 1989, Balmain merging with Western Suburbs wouldn't have even been a thought for a single moment, yet ten years later, the Wests Tigers was conceived. Balmain's only game against Canterbury-Bankstown for the 1999 season was Round 25. Balmain played them twice in 1998, and they split the wins. In 1997 they didn't play each other, as Canterbury-Bankstown was a Super League club. In 1996 Sydney Tigers played them twice and won both games. Sydney/Balmain Tigers had three wins and one loss against Canterbury-Bankstown since the 1996 season, and Parramatta had been in first place on the competition ladder when Balmain beat them during Round 24. Going into the Round 25 game, Canterbury-Bankstown were in sixth place, and with a top-eight finals, a win against Balmain might help them move up the ladder.

Stadium Australia could seat just over one hundred thousand people, in anticipation of the 2000 Summer Olympic Games in Sydney, and even though 21,031 people attended the Round 25 game, which would normally be considered a good crowd for an NRL game, all those empty seats made the venue look sparse that night. With a high-scoring game, all the action on the field provided plenty of entertainment, and combined, both clubs would score twelve tries. Hooker Adam Nable scored the final try of his NRL career, as did centre Craig Hancock, and winger Chris Morcombe had a pair of tries, which became the final points of his NRL career. Nable would make first-grade appearances the next two seasons, but his final career NRL try was scored as a Balmain Tiger. The game got away from Balmain, though, and Canterbury-Bankstown won it 44–24.

For their final NRL game, Balmain made the trip down the Hume Highway to Canberra. Who could have possibly imagined that Balmain's final two NRL games would be played consecutively against the two clubs they had last played in consecutive grand finals? Balmain only had the one fixture against Canberra for the 1999 season, and they hadn't beaten Canberra since Round 9 of the 1992 season, when Balmain won 34–20 at Leichhardt Oval.

Balmain had only played Canberra twice in finals play, and the first time was the 1988 semifinals, with Balmain winning 14–6. Canberra had been grand finalists in 1987, and they finished the 1988 regular season in third place, while Balmain scraped into the top six placed teams 1988 finals format in sixth place. In 1989 Balmain finished the regular season in third place and Canberra finished fourth, but it is often underappreciated that Canberra had a longer journey than Balmain in the top six clubs finals. Canberra had to win three finals games to get to the grand final, while Balmain got there by winning two.

Canberra and Balmain won their respective semifinals, but because Balmain was the higher-placed winner, having finished the regular season in third place, they went straight to the grand final and Canberra had to play the highest-placed semifinal loser in the preliminary final against South Sydney. Canberra won that game 32–16, and if their season hadn't been long enough, playing extra time in the 1989 grand final made it a monumental season for Canberra, which was highlighted with their first grand final win.

For their 1999 Round 26 game, both clubs would wear their 1989 apparel to commemorate the 1989 grand final. Mal Meninga had been Canberra's coach since 1997, and in the 1989 grand final, he played as a centre for them, partnered by Laurie Daley. By Round 26 in 1999, Daley was Canberra's captain and five-eighth, and he was the only player on the ground that had participated in the 1989 grand final.

By 1999 Canberra weren't the power they had once been, and

going into the game, they were in ninth place, just one spot short of the top-eight finals. Balmain had been stuck in fourteenth position for three weeks, despite their Round 24 win over Parramatta. Canberra had to beat Balmain and needed Brisbane to lose in order to finish the regular season in the top eight. As Brisbane had played their Round 26 game on Friday, August 27, against Canterbury-Bankstown and won the game 14–12, the result eliminated Canberra from having any chance of reaching the 1999 finals. So Balmain and Canberra were both playing for pride, but quietly, Balmain fans hoped and begged for a win, because if they won their last NRL game against Canberra, it might just soothe some of the pain of losing the 1989 grand final.

A crowd of 13,617 people watched the game, and they got to see some points scored, but it certainly wasn't Balmain's afternoon, with Canberra winning 42–14. Adam Nable was Balmain's starting hooker for the game, and as he remembers it, "I think we started off strong the first fifteen minutes...then it just got away" (Nable 2018). The result was disappointing, but the game had its own highlights for Balmain. Team captain/lock Darren Senter and his great friend front rower Shane Walker made their one-hundredth Sydney/Balmain Tigers appearances that afternoon.

Chris Morcombe started the game at fullback for Balmain, and it was the only time during his first-grade career he'd wear the number-one jersey. He was Balmain's top try scorer, with nine for the 1999 season, and the game against Canberra was the final appearance he made in first grade. With two first-grade stints at Balmain (1994 and 1999) Morcombe's twenty-two first-grade appearances were all as a Balmain Tiger.

Veteran back Craig Hancock also made his last first-grade appearance that afternoon. He came off the bench against Canberra, and he would finish his career with 192 first-grade appearances. He had started his first-grade career at Manly Warringah in 1989 and stayed there to the end of the 1998 season, yet Hancock had done a commendable job during his season as a Balmain Tiger by adding experience to Balmain's backline, and he was still versatile enough to play wing or centre. Appearing in twenty games for Balmain in 1999, he scored six tries.

Balmain's final NRL game had additional significance for Nathan Webber, as he made his first-grade debut that game. He started the game as a centre, and it would be the only NRL appearance of his career. His older brother Jason was unavailable for the game, but Nathan made Balmain Tigers history as the club's final NRL debutant, and that gave him claim to be the last Balmain Tiger.

That same game, two other players would go on to have their own claims as last NRL Balmain Tigers, as second rower Luke O'Donnell came off the bench against Canberra, as did front rower Kylie Leuluai. O'Donnell was the last Balmain Tiger to appear in the NRL, with his career finishing at the end of the 2013 season. Leuluai made seventy-eight NRL first-grade appearances from 1999 to 2006 before joining the English Super League. From 2007 to 2015 Leuluai would go on to make, incredibly, 266 appearances, all with Leeds Rhinos.

Balmain finished the 1999 season fifteenth of seventeen clubs, and the final two losses of the season ensured they didn't win a single away game that year. Even during Balmain's last place, "wooden spoon" seasons of 1994, 1981, and 1974, they managed to win some away games. Balmain also had a wooden spoon season in 1911, and they won no away games that year, but it should be noted that the regular season consisted of just fourteen games/rounds.

In 1999 the away game that slipped from Balmain's grasp was

Round 19 against South Sydney at the Sydney Football Stadium. Balmain led 12–0 at halftime, but South Sydney scored twenty-two points to nil in the second half to win the game 22–12. Nable was Balmain's hooker for that game. "It's hard…it's so hard to get a win…I bet you Junior [Pearce] would have been pulling his hair out…you look back on the season and say 'that one got away' or 'that one we should have done this'…it's also a disappointing thing when you're playing the house down and you get robbed on [referee] calls, and should have won that one," recalls Nable (2018).

Balmain's 1999 season was distinctive as their final year in the NRL, and the players competed hard against every opponent they played, regardless of the final score. For Nable, "It's a privilege…I'm honoured to have played for the Balmain Tigers," (Nable 2018) and that sentiment would surely be shared among so many of his 1999 teammates. Great friendships were made as a Balmain Tiger for Joel Caine, who said, "There wouldn't be too many weeks that go past if I haven't spoken with Mick [Michael] Gillett and Mark O'Neill, that would be the number one highlight [from 1999] for sure… John Carlaw and Adam Nable, another two I keep in touch with, they're great fellas" (Caine 2018).

The process of Balmain and Western Suburbs carrying out their joint venture would begin in 1999, yet even though both clubs' seasons had finished and their NRL standalone identities would be gone at the completion of Round 26, 1999 still had one more big surprise. The rest of the calendar year would have some highlights off the field, too, but as the years would pass, more would become clear about what merging the two clubs had achieved. Close to three months had passed since the special general meetings on July 27, when members of Balmain Tigers and Western Suburbs Magpies had overwhelmingly voted for a joint venture between the

two clubs, which had guaranteed them a licence in the rationalised fourteen-club NRL competition for the year 2000. The NRL
publicly announced the clubs approved for the fourteen-club competition on October 15, but the already merged St. George Illawarra Dragons club had been guaranteed a place, so in fact, there
were only thirteen licences available. The NRL criteria findings had
ranked the clubs as follows: (1) Brisbane Broncos, (2) Newcastle
Knights, (3) Melbourne Storm, (4) Canterbury-Bankstown Bulldogs, (5) Cronulla-Sutherland Sharks, (6) Sydney City Roosters,
(7) Parramatta Eels, (8) North Queensland Cowboys, (9) Canberra
Raiders, (10) Auckland Warriors, (11) Manly Warringah Sea Eagles, (12) Penrith Panthers, (13) Balmain Tigers, (14) North Sydney Bears, (15) Western Suburbs Magpies, and (16) South Sydney
Rabbitohs. Balmain had qualified for the final licence, yet they were
already committed and approved as the joint venture Wests Tigers.

The fact that Balmain could have stood alone was not a straightforward situation, because the decision to merge the club had been
significantly prompted by the possibility that they wouldn't meet
the criteria, and the joint venture was regarded as a high-percent-
age strategy that offered a future, which the NRL then guaranteed.
It would have been a huge gamble to wait out the NRL's criteria
findings, yet as it turned out, Balmain had secured the final licence,
which confirmed how close they were to not getting approved. According to club CEO Danny Munk,

> The management team put together a fairly detailed docu-
> ment what our answers were to the criteria…our problem was
> if we had gotten in there was no guarantee there was a long
> term future because the cost of the game was getting to such
> a point that our financial viability was not something I could
> plan out over the next five years…our big risk was that we

could have got in and there was no additional grant money… all the player payments (salaries) had gone up exponentially because all the player managers were going "Oh you've got a new competition, you've got a new media grant therefore the salaries have got to be X"…You suddenly found yourself facing a business plan where any grant money that you got from the NRL was going one hundred percent to player payments…an absolutely unsustainable model…the fact was there was things such as Leichhardt Oval [needed work and capital to pay for it]…we knew how much money had to be spent on Leichhardt [Oval] and it wasn't capital we had…We could have gone and taken a punt and stood on our own but it wouldn't necessarily have guaranteed a future…Our fear was "yes" we would get in for 2000, but would we still be there in 2005, if we couldn't be a financially competitive team? (Munk 2018)

Despite the safety the joint venture offered, it didn't sit well with some Balmain fans that the club had effectively waived the opportunity to stand alone. A frustrating point was that the club didn't even need to wait ninety days to find out the NRL criteria findings, and would it have been so detrimental to wait? Some Balmain fans take the view that the club could have stood alone and developed new business models to meet the costs of being an NRL club. Theoretically, it was a possibility, and perhaps a wealthy businessperson could have eventually become a private owner or there could have even been a consortium of owners.

What Balmain definitely lost as a result of amalgamating before October 15 was bargaining power. Had they pursued a merge partner after the criteria findings announcement, Balmain could have negotiated stronger terms for the club with a prospective partner, or they could have made a joint venture a medium- or long-term plan, and thus given themselves more time to plan and integrate a new structure.

There was a radical view among some fans of the club that Balmain could have back-flipped on their joint venture agreement, but this would have likely resulted in litigation from the NRL and Western Suburbs. Plus, the club would have surely been suspended from participating in the 2000 NRL competition if they had back-flipped.

Balmain's board of directors, though, had business integrity, and they were committed to seeing the merger through. Looking back on it, "'99 was a hard year but the highlights were how the management board worked together...that process of getting the joint venture through the way that we did...we had to put together a business plan and presented it to the NRL, and got the NRL's support...getting two community groups, Wests and us, to agree on a go-forward, and putting the plan together, implementing that, and getting a team ready by the end of '99 for 2000...For me 2005 [Wests Tigers' grand final win] was the true celebration of that... it was a continuance of the history of the Tigers and Wests, and the continuance of that tradition...for me it justified everything we did in '99...Wests and the Tigers brand is a very strong product... Twenty years down the track the Tigers brand is alive and well...If we hadn't done what we did in '99 I'm not sure that brand would still exist," said Munk (2018).

What is often forgotten is that when the NRL criteria findings were announced in October 1999, the general public reaction was not particularly focused on Balmain having been able to stand alone; rather, South Sydney fans and their club were up in arms that they would not be part of the 2000 NRL competition. They would take to the streets, protest-marching against the NRL, and they would take the matter to court. North Sydney didn't have the "people power" South Sydney had, yet they would have some voice regarding the NRL's decision not to grant them a licence, too. Through court action, South Sydney would get back into the NRL for the 2002 season, and there is still some glimmer of hope that one day North Sydney may return to the NRL as the Central Coast Bears.

As Balmain would exist as part of a joint venture club, it hadn't been completely lost to the sport, and the view that the Balmain Tigers and Western Suburbs Magpies were the parents of Wests Tigers provided some comfort with what the two clubs created. There were some supporters of both clubs, though, who didn't embrace Wests Tigers, and their interest ended with the loss of the teams they had followed. For many others, Wests Tigers was a fresh start and the club was still connected to its past, which made for a simple transition.

A sense of having lost Balmain was therefore not totally apparent, because it was a partner in a club and the Tigers name would go on. But then there was a loss, and it was completely unexpected. On February 2, 2000, Balmain's number-one fan, Laurie Nichols, passed away at seventy-nine years old. He was attending a charity fundraising event when he died from a ruptured stomach ulcer. February 2 was a Wednesday, and Wests Tigers played their maiden game on February 6, which was a Sunday. Nichols had stated he wasn't in favour of the joint venture, and some might say that he passed on forever a Balmain Tigers man.

His legacy to the club was his energetic and passionate support of the team through good and bad times and braving all variants of weather wearing a Balmain singlet. No other NRL club had a fan like him, and his rhymes, war cries, and shadowboxing on the sidelines of the field as Balmain played made him a part of the game. If people hadn't realised or fully accepted that regardless of how much of the Wests Tigers joint venture Balmain formed, they were nevertheless no longer a standalone NRL club. The death of Nichols embodied that things would never be the same again.

In terms of NRL game play, the transition from Balmain Tigers to Wests Tigers was just 161 days. Balmain had played their final NRL game on August 29, 1999, and Wests Tigers played their first on February 6, 2000. From July 27, 1999, just over six months had passed, and the new club had been born and had taken to the field. As much as the joint venture was embraced and nurtured by those that played a part in constructing it, they never forgot their roots, and that was certainly the case for Balmain Tigers CEO Danny Munk. "That whole experience with Balmain was certainly a highlight for me. I don't regret one minute there; sometimes it was pretty tough, but those years certainly have a great fondness for me," said Munk (2018).

The Balmain Tigers was a foundation club of the NSWRFL, and for ninety-two seasons they were part of the league, which would take on different names and also expand well outside of New South Wales. The 1999 Balmain Tigers would be the last to play at NRL level, and interestingly, more players appeared in first grade during the 1999 season than any other year, with forty players appearing across their twenty-four-game season. Some context needs to be given to the fact that the length of the competition evolved over time, as during the first season in 1908 it was a nine-game regular season. For the ten years from 1990 to 1999, Balmain/Sydney Tigers played twenty-two regular-season games for eight of those years; they played twenty-four in both 1998 and 1999.

For the most part, about thirty players appeared each year in first grade from 1990 to 1999 (1990, 31 players; 1991, 34; 1992, 32; 1993, 33; 1994, 38; 1995, 33; 1996, 32; 1997, 30; 1998, 29; and 1999, 40). There were some reasonable factors that explained why 1999 had the highest number of players to appear, with forty, which included player injuries, and it was one of only two seasons with the most regular-season games played, with twenty-four.

As a club and playing group, those forty players were the last Balmain Tigers to play NRL first grade. They were Joel Caine, John Carlaw, Ben Duckworth, Shayne Dunley, Craig Field, Ben Galea, James Gannon, Michael Gillett, Craig Hancock, Solomon Haumono, Hayes Lauder, Kylie Leuluai, Jason Lowrie, Mark Luland, Brendan Magnus, Andrew Meads, Laloa Milford, Chris Morcombe, Adam Nable, Shannon Nevin, Luke O'Donnell, Mark O'Neill, Michael Ostini, Steven Price, Wade Rothery, Darren Senter, Nick Shaw, Jacin Sinclair, Brad Smith, Tyran Smith, Adam Starr, Mark Stimson, Richard Villasanti, Shane Walker, Jason Webber, Nathan Webber, James Webster, Garth Wood, Troy Wozniak, and Justin Yeo.

The 1999 season may not have been the ending Balmain predicted or hoped for, yet there were forty players who wore the black and orange club colours for Balmain's final NRL season. For some players it was the club they made their NRL first-grade debut with, and for others it would be the only season they appeared in first grade. Then there were those that ended their careers as a 1999 Balmain Tiger, and for others 1999 was part of a much longer career. Being a member of that final team meant different things to each player, yet they all shared that, together, they were the last "Balmain Boys," proud and determined teammates on the 1999 Balmain Tigers.

# ABOUT THE AUTHOR

Nicholas Henning has always enjoyed telling a story and aims to be informative and entertaining with all his works. He likes to offer a unique mix of history, sociology, and anthropology, making his narratives unlike any other. He has also written fiction titles and a memoir covering the first twenty years of his life.

Also by Nicholas Henning:

*Brennan Cooper*

*The American Dream: From Perth to Sacramento*

*The Tourist*

*Boomerang Baseball*

*Aussies in the Majors*

*Aussie Baseball Musings*

*Henning's Story from 1979 to 1999: A Memoir of Ideas and
    Inspirations*

*Aussie World Baseball Classic Experiences from 2006 to 2017*

*Retro Balmain Tigers*

# REFERENCES

Ackland, John, email message to author, October 28, 2018. (A special thank you to Stephen Purcell for referring me to John.)

Barrack, Mark. "Obituary – Mata'itai Savaii Savea." *1998 Auckland Rugby League Yearbook*. Auckland: Milestone, 1997–98. (A special thank you to Greg Whaiapu and Selwyn Pearson from Auckland Rugby League for locating and providing a copy of this record.)

Caine, Joel, in discussion with the author, on October 29, 2018. (A special thank you to Steve Gillis for introducing me to Joel.)

Dollin, Shawn, Andrew Ferguson, and Bill Bates. Rugby League Project. (For all player data/statistics and game-day details.)

Elias, Ben. *Balmain Benny: The Stormy League Career of Ben Elias*. With Ian Heads. Randwick, Australia: Ironbark Press, 1993.

Knight, Richard. "Promising League Player and Mate Perish Fishing." *New Zealand Herald*. January 1999.

Munk, Danny, in discussion with the author, on October 29, 2018.

Nable, Adam, in discussion with the author, on October 15, 2018.

*New Zealand Herald*. "Heroic Action Cost Life." January 1999.

Pearce, Wayne, in discussion with the author, on November 3, 2018.

Roach, Steve. *Doing My Block*. With Ray Chesterton. Randwick, Australia: Ironbark Press, 1992.

Sironen, Paul. *Sirro! Tales from Tiger Town*. With Daniel Lane. Sydney: Australian Broadcasting Corporation Books, 1997.

Printed in Great Britain
by Amazon

85110295R00084